Treating Depression
Using Cognitive Behavioral
Therapy Skills and Interventions

Books in This Series

Crisis Intervention for Community Behavioral Health Service Providers in Ohio

Overcoming Reluctance in Therapeutic Relationships

Psychotherapy for Families

Therapeutic Behavioral Services Using Interventions Based on Principles and Techniques of Cognitive Behavioral Therapy

Treating Attention Deficit Hyperactivity Disorder, Impulsivity, and Disruptive Behaviors in Children Using Behavioral Skill Building and Cognitive Behavioral Therapy Skills and Interventions

Treating Anxiety Using Cognitive Behavioral Therapy Skills and Interventions

Treating Depression Using Cognitive Behavioral Therapy Skills and Interventions

Treating Posttraumatic Stress Disorder Using Cognitive Behavioral Therapy Skills and Interventions

Treating Depression
Using Cognitive Behavioral Therapy Skills and Interventions

TREATMENT AND INTERVENTION MANUAL

Reinhild Boehme, LISW-S

Benjamin Kearney, PhD, *series editor*

THE INSTITUTE OF
FAMILY & COMMUNITY
IMPACT

An OhioGuidestone Company
Berea, Ohio

Nothing contained in the manual is, or should be considered or used as, a substitute for medical advice, diagnosis, or treatment. The manual is not intended to replace, and does not replace, the specialized training and professional judgment of a health care or mental health care professional. Individuals should seek the advice of a physician or other health care provider with any questions regarding medications, personal health or medical conditions. This manual has been prepared as a tool to assist providers. In its efforts to provide information that is accurate and generally in accord with the standards of practice at the time of publication, the author has checked with sources believed to be reliable. However, in view of the possibility of human error or changes in behavioral, mental health, or medical sciences, neither the author, nor the editor and publisher, nor any other party who has been involved in the preparation or publication of this work warrants that the information contained herein is in every respect accurate or complete, and they are not responsible for any errors or omissions, or the results obtained from the use of such information. Further, the information presented in this manual does not constitute legal or financial advice or opinions. The ultimate responsibility for correct billing lies with the provider of the services. The reader should consult the current version of the relevant laws, regulations, and rulings.

The Institute of Family and Community Impact
An OhioGuidestone Company
www.OhioGuidestone.org

ISBN 978-1-7328190-8-5
Printed in the United States of America

Contents

Preface

For mental health professionals, building trusting relationships with clients and knowing which interventions will most benefit them are challenging enough. Helping clients who are also dealing at the same time with chronic conditions such as poverty, violence, and addiction can seem overwhelming. That's especially true for behavioral health service providers who have limited experience. That's why we at OhioGuidestone have developed this series of clinical manuals to help professionals develop their skills while providing effective treatment.

OhioGuidestone, the largest community behavioral health organization in Ohio, regularly trains new therapists and other behavioral health interventionists to work with clients who face severe, therapy-interfering challenges. We've brought that experience to these manuals.

In this era of managed care oversight, tight funding, and pressure to deliver evidence-based or informed care, it is essential for new therapists to get up to speed on best practices quickly. It is also essential for experienced clinicians to be well provided with effective and varied treatment plans. The manuals in this series provide step-by-step guidance on evidence-based and informed treatment modalities and interventions that can be used by both licensed and unlicensed mental health professionals—as well as by their supervisors for training purposes.

Seasoned mental health professionals will find the resources offered in these manuals useful for developing a renewed focus on evidence- and research-based interventions. At OhioGuidestone, our interventions are grounded in cognitive behavioral science and also shaped by the relational and attachment scientific advances that continue to inform the behavioral health field (especially the interpersonal neurobiology work published by W. W. Norton & Company). We understand the demands of serving client populations experiencing trauma and toxic stress. Our interventions are designed not to address discrete diagnoses (clients often have more than one) but rather the symptoms that are related to them. The series addresses a wide range of issues, such as depression, anxiety, ADHD, PTSD, and even reluctance to engage in therapy, and it provides interventions for children and adults.

We cannot "fix" our clients. But we can guide them along clear paths toward developing the skills they need to navigate the challenges they face, in their thoughts and in their lives. It's our sincere hope that the books in this series will help better prepare more mental health professionals to do just that.

— Benjamin Kearney, PhD, series editor

If you purchased this manual and want to make copies of interventions to help your clients, please do so. However, please do not share copies with other professionals but encourage them to buy manuals for themselves. This will help us continue to add to and update this series, to better equip all helpers who make a difference.

Introduction

This manual is for licensed mental health providers who provide psychotherapy and related services.

Treating depressed clients, whether they are children or adults, can feel like an overwhelming task. There is usually so much to do: Our clients may have lost the ability to do things for themselves, to "have a life." They may not leave their homes, they may eat poorly and suffer from physical ailments such as hypertension or diabetes. Children may learn poorly and miss a lot of school due to depression, physical illness, and family difficulties.

Learning About the Treatment of Depression

If you are looking for a book specifically outlining cognitive-behavioral therapy (CBT) for depression, you may want to read *Essential Components of Cognitive-Behavior Therapy for Depression* by Jacqueline B. Persons, Joan Davidson, and Michael A. Tompkins (2000). If you would like a very brief and concise introduction to this topic, read *Cognitive Behavioral Therapy for Depression* by Mark Fefergrad and Ari Zaretsky (2013). This book includes a laminated pull-out practice reminder card as well as a DVD with examples, including client role play.

If you would like a more in-depth overview of the theoretical foundations of CBT, as well as step-by step practice guidelines integrated with case examples, you may want to read Deborah and Keith Dobson's *Evidence-Based Practice of Cognitive Behavioral Therapy* (2016) or *Doing CBT: A Comprehensive Guide to Working with Behaviors, Thoughts, and Emotions* by David Tolin (2016).

Why Cognitive Behavioral Therapy?

CBT offers a structured approach to treatment. This can create a counterweight to the heaviness of depression. When there seems no way out and change seems impossible, CBT always offers a next step, because it insists on clear goals, a structure for each session, and a structure for the course of treatment.

CBT is evidence based. The Society for Clinical Psychology identifies behavior therapy and cognitive therapy as having strong research support for the treatment of depression. *The Practitioner's Guide to Evidence-Based Psychotherapy* (Fisher & O'Donohue, 2006) notes that CBT is evidence based and supported (p. 242).

CBT: The Essential Elements

CBT focuses on addressing the three elements of the *cognitive triad*: thoughts (also known as cognitions), feelings (also known as emotions), and behaviors. Note that in CBT, this is called the cognitive triad, rather than the feelings or emotional triad.

CBT holds that all kinds of problems, including behavioral or emotional problems, are rooted in unrealistic and faulty thinking. Hence, unrealistic and faulty thinking must be identified and corrected.

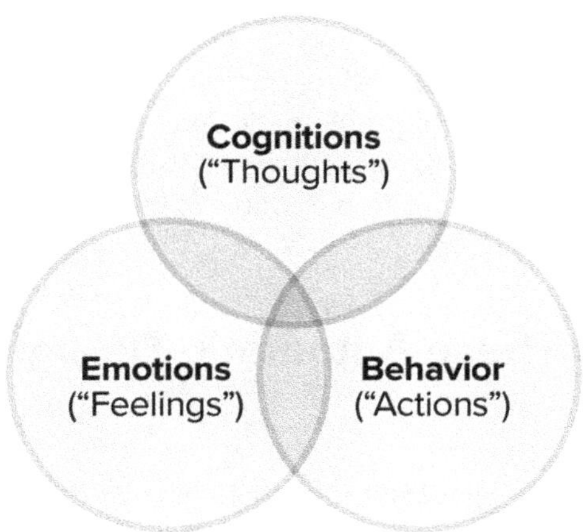

Figure 1

This conceptualization contains three components:

- The emotional component
- The behavioral component
- The cognitive component

These three interact with each other. Thoughts, especially *automatic thoughts,* or thoughts that just "happen"—Tolin (2016) calls them "interpretations, because they usually interpret what is happening in some unpleasant way"—impact behaviors and emotions. But behaviors also impact emotions and cognitions.

What Exactly Do We Mean When We Talk About the Cognitive Component?

What and how we think impacts how we feel and what we do. But do we always know what we are thinking? Beck, Rush, Shaw, and Emery (1979) observed "the depressed person's tendency to interpret his ongoing experiences in a negative way" (p. 11). These interpretations then shape the way the depressed person narrates his life. Beck used the metaphor of an intercom to bring this internal chatter into the therapeutic conversation. He named this uninvited, ever-present chatter automatic thoughts. These are the thoughts we did not ask for and are often only somewhat aware of.

Here are some examples of automatic thoughts:

- I always mess everything up.

- She hates me.

- I am going to fail this one.

Notice that automatic thoughts are judgmental in nature. They don't often compliment us. If they do, they are not problematic and seldom a topic in treatment. It would be a good idea, however, to track the transformation from negative automatic thoughts to more realistic thoughts in the course of treatment.

But Where Do These Automatic Thoughts Come From?

In CBT, basic negative views of self, others, and the world are called core beliefs or schemas. We may hold these beliefs without being aware of them. They drive how we think about ourselves, consciously and unconsciously (internal chatter), and how we think of each other and the world. Automatic thoughts are rooted in core beliefs, and we generally are not aware of the core beliefs we hold.

Here are some examples of core beliefs:

- I am unworthy.

- I am a failure.

- I am unlovable.

These, of course, are examples of unhealthy core beliefs. Here are some examples of healthy core beliefs:

- I am worthy.

- I am capable.

- I am lovable.

Where, then, do these core beliefs come from?

CBT insists on a focus on the here and now. We may never know where our core beliefs come from. Or we may know, but we cannot deconstruct them by simply knowing who to blame for our core negative core beliefs. Yes, perhaps a parent instilled a sense of worthlessness that led to a core belief of unworthiness. But CBT is what Tolin (2016) calls "present oriented" (p. 8). It is not that CBT discredits what has happened to a client or disregards the emotional pain that lingers. Rather, CBT insists that the client move into the here and now. The question to our client then becomes:

- *What do you think/believe about what happened to you?*

- *Are there other, more realistic and accurate ways of thinking about the past/the impact of the past?*

In other words, faulty core beliefs and negative automatic thoughts can be corrected here and now.

Here is an example of what correcting faulty thinking about past hurt might look like:

- Your client was neglected by her parents and emotionally and sexually abused. She holds the core belief that she is "ruined for life." Her automatic thoughts about the past tell her that she is "dirty" and that no one would want her. CBT would acknowledge the hurt but move towards correcting those faulty automatic thoughts using evidence from the here and now.

CBT insists that we rationally tackle faulty core beliefs *now*, that the core belief must be examined using empirical methods (evidence), and then adjusted to a more realistic core belief. More adaptive and realistic core beliefs then lead to more adaptive and realistic thoughts that correct negative automatic thoughts. More realistic thoughts about self, other, and the world lead to behaviors that are a better fit for reality and hence produce a better outcome.

So here is how thoughts (cognitions) are viewed in CBT:

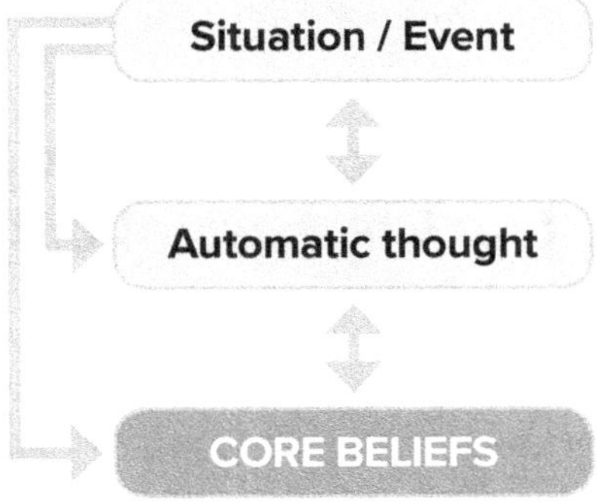

Figure 2: Note that core beliefs are much harder to identify than automatic thoughts. Automatic thoughts just appear: we do not have to ask for them. Because they appear so often, they are easier to bring into conscious awareness.

An event or situation triggers a core belief. The core belief results in negative automatic thoughts. These negative automatic thoughts lead to behaviors that are not a good "fit" with the situation, because they are based on faulty interpretations of what is actually going on.

Here is an example of what this may look like:

> Jason is having an argument with his partner. As soon as the disagreement begins, he hears himself saying to himself: "Stupid, I am so stupid." This automatic thought is rooted in Jason's core belief that he is unlovable. He developed this core belief as a young child due to ongoing emotional neglect. Jason is overwhelmed by both sadness and anger (the emotional component of the cognitive triad) and lashes out at his partner, then leaves, intending to never return (the behavioral component of the triad).

What went wrong?

Jason did not assess the situation accurately. He is clearly not "stupid" (finished high school, works as a mechanic). But he does have a core belief that he is unlovable (clearly also not true, as he is currently in a loving relationship). He reacts emotionally to his negative automatic thoughts, and his actions are based on the intense emotions of sadness and anger.

The key in Jason's treatment is to get him away from faulty interpretations and into more accurate interpretations of what is truly happening right now. Here is what that might look like:

> Jason is having an argument with his partner. They disagree, and it is difficult for him to accept that they are in disagreement. Jason comes to understand that disagreements are a normal part of any relationship. He recognizes his sadness about having a disagreement, but he moves past this and tries to work out a compromise with his partner. When he reaches a compromise with his partner he feels validated and competent.

If you find yourself repeatedly talking with your client about a pesky automatic thought, you may be on to a core belief.

What About Behaviors? What Do We Mean When We Refer to the Behavioral Component of Depression?

Inaccurate core beliefs lead to inaccurate automatic thoughts about a situation. These automatic, negative and rapid-fire thoughts lead to behavioral responses that are based on a faulty assessment of the situation. If I assume that things will go wrong no matter what I do, my assessment of the future will be negative, and I will feel no need to act purposefully and consciously. There may be no need to act at all. I am helpless and hopeless.

Helplessness and hopelessness are key features of depression. Why should I act if nothing matters? Why should I act if everything I do goes wrong? Inaction, then, is at the core of depression. Inaction feeds into an ongoing faulty assessment of the present through more negative automatic thoughts, leading to increasingly overwhelming feelings of helplessness and hopelessness.

Note that a main behavioral component of depression is inaction based on feelings of helplessness and hopelessness. This behavioral component can easily "flip" into aggression (a rebellion against the feeling of helplessness). It is important to understand that aggression can be and often is an expression of depression, especially in children.

Behaviors based on a faulty interpretation of self, others, and the world maintain depression. In order for us to address depression, behaviors have to change. In CBT this is called *behavioral activation*. When using behavioral activation, we help our clients realize that "doing better in order to feel better" (Tolin, 2016, p. 39) can work.

Here is how behavioral components relate of the cognitive components of depression:

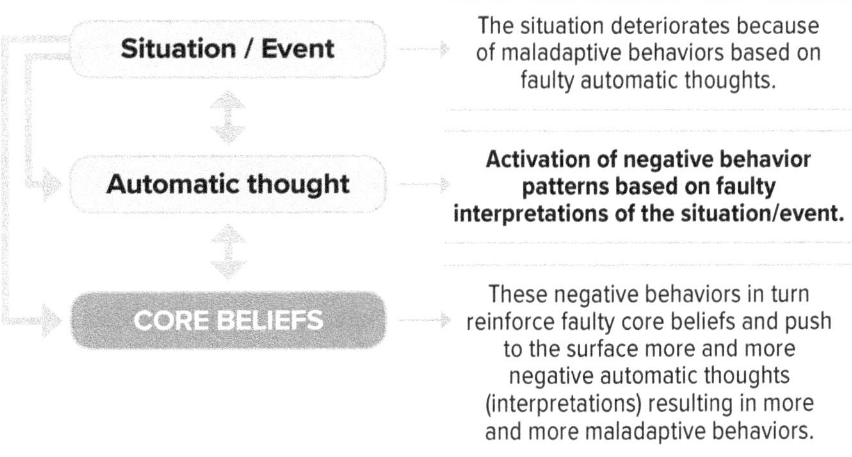

Figure 3

What About the Emotional Component of the Cognitive Triad?

What are emotions? Why do we have them? Do they serve a basic purpose?

Tolin (2016) acknowledges that there are basic human emotions that are biologically based. They have a function. Fear, for example, evolutionarily speaking, is meant to keep us alive. So is love. He differentiates between "physiological sensations" (p. 81) and "subjective emotional states." In other words, there are basic emotions that we need. They keep us alive. Davis, Panksepp, and Solms (2018) have identified seven primary emotions that help us survive. And to be alive means to be connected with others. Depression is so damaging because it severs our connection with others as well as our connections with our primary emotions that keep us alive. When we are depressed, we no longer seek out new and enriching experiences or the company of others.

Beck, Rush, Shaw, and Emery (1979) assert that depression leads us to not fully experience, or not experience at all, the basic feelings of love and joy. Nothing is left, then, but unpleasant or seemingly intolerable emotional experiences such as rage, anger, and despair.

Depression makes us feel alone—even if we are not alone. Neurobiologically, in order to be well, we need to be connected to a caring community.

When this connection is broken or feels broken (as it does in depression), our emotions become a "subjective emotional state" (Tolin, 2016), disconnected from a collective emotional state and further reinforcing loneliness and helplessness. Narvaez (2014) outlines the ways in which individual and collective emotional states and social norms (or lack thereof) are connected by a foundation of appropriate child-rearing practices that foster close attachment relationships. Inadequate child-rearing practices, on the other hand, can reinforce the notion that ultimately one is all alone and must fend for oneself with others standing in the way of gaining access to resources. It is easy to see how the latter produces an ethic only focused on oneself rather than oneself as part of a community.

Emotions are impacted by physiological states. A racing heart can trigger the emotion of fear. But a racing heart can also trigger the subjective emotional state of depression.

If, for example, I fear my heart racing, I may avoid anything that raises my heart rate and feel depressed about my perceived inability to be physically active. The feeling of fear and the inaccurate assessment of reality (assuming that nothing is medically wrong) is pushing me into inactivity, which in turn makes me feel like a failure (automatic thought leading to feelings of failure). Feeling like a failure makes me less likely to become active again. I now sit at home, feeling like a failure, and tell myself that I am failure. I fail to take action because my assessment is that nothing I do will make a difference.

Emotions, behaviors, and automatic thoughts (and ultimately core beliefs) are intimately connected, always interacting with each other. Emotions can be incredibly adaptive when they move us into the right kind of action. Here is an example: If someone in my family dies, I will naturally feel sad. There may be, for some time, a physical feeling of heaviness or, in the case of a sudden and unexpected loss, a sense of shock. This feeling of heaviness and sadness is meant, neurobiologically, to send me back into the company of others—my family or my friends.

If I reconnect with my group because I am sad, the sadness is adaptive. If I stay in extended isolation, my sadness may increase, turning into depression and the feeling that no one can understand. If no one understands me, then there is no need to go out and connect with others. I am alone in my suffering. Surely this feeling reinforces my depression.

So here is how the emotional components of depression relate to the behavioral and cognitive components:

Figure 4

CBT in Action: How to Conceptualize a Case

CBT offers a clear path to treatment. After a thorough assessment, you must develop a clear *case formulation* (Dobson & Dobson, 2017). Tolin (2016) calls this a "meaty conceptualization" (p. 94) of your case. In other words: We must create a hypothesis of what is creating and maintaining the problem.

Once you have completed your case conceptualization, you are ready to identify your intervention targets and create a treatment plan.

But before you do so, you must put your case conceptualization on paper. Where does it go?

- Your case conceptualization belongs in the clinical summary section of the diagnostic evaluation in the client record. When you write your clinical summary, be sure to include the behavioral, emotional, and cognitive elements that create and maintain your client's problems. Name the problems that you want to target for your client. The problems you have identified become the basis of your treatment plan.

Let's walk through a case:

Case Vignette: Heather

Heather is a 27-year-old single mother with two young children living in public housing. Heather lost her job 2 months ago. Since then, she has not paid rent. She finds herself unable to take any action. She has no energy and has gained a tremendous amount of weight. Heather spends much of her time sleeping or watching television, neglecting her children's emotional needs. She has no energy to play with them or assist with homework. Heather knows she should see a doctor about her diabetes but can't see herself getting to the clinic and explains that she has no bus money.

Heather feels hopeless about her situation and her whole life. She no longer speaks to her mother or her friends, as she is embarrassed about her life. She has considered taking pills to end her life but is holding off because she does not want her children to suffer. Heather feels like she has failed her children and herself and is a disappointment to her family.

Heather's needs are many. Where should you start?

Heather's case is not an uncommon one. Our clients are often faced with multiple barriers, many of which are beyond their control. Let's call them *therapy-interfering conditions*. Here are some examples: of therapy-interfering conditions:

- Poverty
- Lack of education
- Incarceration of a family member
- Disability
- Racism
- Sexism

While our clients are faced with these conditions (they did not choose them), they are forced to deal with them. There is ample evidence that conditions of toxic stress, especially in childhood, can contribute to the development of physical and mental illness. For more information about the impact of adverse childhood experiences on the development of physical and mental illness, please refer to the ACEs Too High website at www.acestoohigh.com.

How can CBT be helpful when there are therapy-interfering conditions present?

- CBT can help correct automatic thoughts of self-blame about conditions beyond the client's control.
- CBT can help the client focus on taking action. Moving into action can take many forms, one of them being advocating for social justice.
- CBT can help the client take action for herself, moving from helplessness to a sense of self-efficacy.

Community Mental Health Practice Alert

What about the conditions many of our clients live in? What about poverty?

Heather lives in poverty, as many of our clients do. She has few external resources. She does not have a car. She does not have savings. Her support system is crumbling. Access to healthy foods is limited.

Your case conceptualization must incorporate the conditions Heather lives in. They have shaped her way of thinking and being and her way of responding to her depression.

Incorporating conditions of toxic stress into the case conceptualization models for Heather that not everything is her fault. It also incorporates a behavioral component into Heather's treatment. When Heather is ready to do so, she may want to take value-based action and develop or increase her advocacy for herself and others living in poverty.

In other words: Heather will learn to take action again. Taking action to create change is a behavior we want to increase through the use of CBT. Keep in mind that the behavior of taking action will have to be modeled and taught.

In other words: Not taking action in an inherent component of depression, it is a symptom that can be treated and changed, but Heather will need your help with this.

Let's try this for our client Heather:

Heather: Assessment and Case Conceptualization/ Problem Identification

Use parts 1 and 2 of the Diagnostic Evaluation. Include information about Heather's socioeconomic status.

Here is what your clinical summary (case conceptualization) may look like:

> Heather's depressive thoughts, feelings, and behaviors were initially triggered by the loss of her job a few months ago.
>
> Heather began to feel like a disappointment to her family and like a failure in life. She now feels that she has no energy. Heather withdrew from her family and friends, seeking to avoid further feelings of failure and disappointment, which reinforced her feelings of loneliness and hopelessness. Heather rarely engages with her children (other than providing for basic needs), and when she does so, it does not give her pleasure.
>
> Heather is avoiding anything that may remind her of what has gone wrong (such as looking at her mail) in order to avoid further feelings of shame and hopelessness about her situation. Heather does not take care of her body. She rarely changes/washes her clothes. Heather has not seen a doctor for a very long time in spite of having been diagnosed with diabetes in the past. Heather eats poorly and does not take her diabetes medication.
>
> Furthermore, Heather is impacted by experiences of toxic stress, namely poverty leading to a lack of external resources as well as a struggle to access the resources that are available. This, in turn, reinforces her hopelessness.

> Heather's hopelessness has reached a level that triggered thoughts of wanting to escape through suicide using old medication, though she currently denies any intent to commit suicide.
>
> Heather's cognitive processes are focused on hopelessness, helplessness, and shame, which are reinforced daily by negative self-talk (automatic thoughts) and inactivity.
>
> Heather meets criteria for major depressive disorder with a qualifier of moderate.
>
> Problems:
>
> Cognitive: Attention focused on hopelessness, hence thoughts of suicide as escape, must address first—possible safety issue.
>
> Behavioral: Basic self-care is lacking—poor nutrition, sleeping too much, poor hygiene, not taking care of fundamentals (may become homeless), lack of interaction with her children.
>
> Emotional: Sadness, hopelessness, shame.

Note that the problem list does not encompass all of Heather's problems, but rather focuses on what is most important—keeping Heather alive (so treatment can continue and she can get better). Additionally, we would want to focus on the behavioral components of treatment first. Better sleep, nutrition, and medical care, and improved stability, are likely to impact Heather's depressive symptoms.

You have completed your case conceptualization. This is a good time to check with your client.

Ask questions like these:

- *Did I get this right?*
- *Is there anything I left out?*
- *Is there anything I need to add?*

Make sure that you are working collaboratively with your client on identifying problems and treatment goals. While CBT can be more directive than other forms of therapy, collaboration ensures that a therapeutic alliance and a "joint ownership" are built (Dobson & Dobson, 2017, p. 53). A solid therapeutic alliance, client and therapist ownership of the case formulation, problem identification, and treatment planning form the basis for treatment success.

What Can Happen If You Don't Work Collaboratively?

If you don't work collaboratively, treatment success is jeopardized from the start. You may think that you understand your client's basic problems. You may have a great case conceptualization in mind, and you may even be correct. But if your client disagrees with you, he may never fully participate in treatment. Any goals you may have established may be partially irrelevant to him; thus, he may not be committed to the course of treatment you are thinking about, and treatment success becomes questionable.

How can you ensure that you are working collaboratively with your client?

- Frequently ask questions like this: *Did I get this right? Is there anything you want to add? What part of what I am saying does not sit right with you?*

- If your client is not ready for the kind of change you have in mind, go back to basics. Ask the miracle question: *If you had one wish and it would come true tomorrow morning, what would your wish be?* (Jong & Berg, 2013). Build collaboration based on that wish.

- Understand that it is your responsibility to build the foundation for collaboration and trust, and that you will have to model them.

Assessment of what specifically impacts your client and causes depressive symptoms should encompass all three aspects: thoughts, feelings, and behaviors. Assessment should be collaborative and structured. Assessment should utilize valid standardized measures and should lead to a case formulation laid out in the clinical summary of the Diagnostic Evaluation in Evolv. The clinical summary concludes with an identification of problems (in order of importance).

Once problems have been identified collaboratively, the treatment plan can be completed.

Here is a visual representation of the assessment process:

Life story
Social conditions
Thoughts Feelings Behaviors
Diagnostic Evaluation Parts 1 and 2
Case conceptualization & identification of problems
Documented in clinical summary in the diagnostic evaluation
Treatment planning
Problems become goals

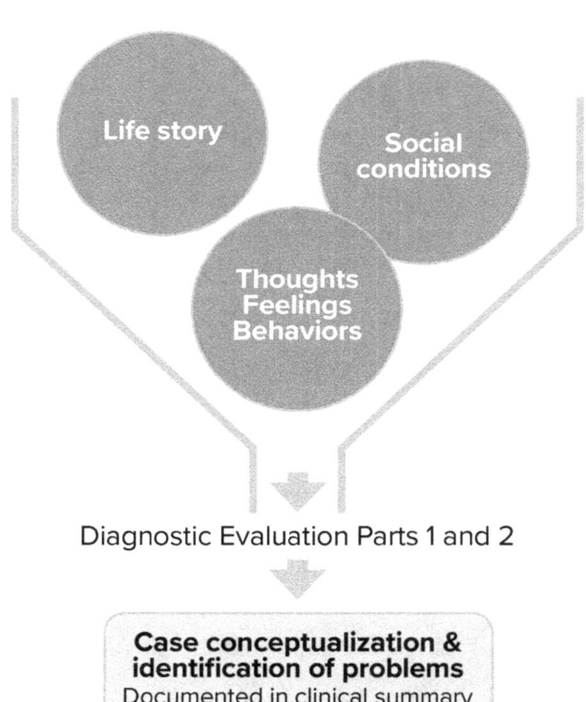

Figure 5

A Word About Suicide and Safety Planning

In her diagnostic evaluation, Heather reports some thoughts of suicide and possible access to means (pills). Her mention of this warrants further questioning and immediate safety planning. You should not wait to create a safety plan until treatment planning begins, because treatment planning could potentially take place at a later date thus putting the client at risk.

If your client discusses thoughts of suicide, complete a formalized suicide risk assessment . Do so in a caring and compassionate manner, explaining that you are asking your client these questions because you want her to be well. Document completion of a formal suicide risk assessment in your case note and ensure that the suicide risk assessment is scanned into the client's electronic record.

Once you have completed the formalized suicide risk assessment, you will in all likelihood need to complete a safety plan. **Any safety concerns about a client must also be reported and discussed with your supervisor on the day that they occur.**

What Is the Function of a Safety Plan?

Tolin (2016) rightfully points out that safety planning in no way guarantees that your client will not harm herself. A safety plan denotes to both you and the client the importance of the matter and specifically the importance of taking action.

By collaboratively creating a safety plan with your client you are:

- Expressing genuine concern and compassion for your client. You are expressing that you value your client as a human being and you want her to stay alive so she can create the life she wants.

- Modeling immediately the importance of taking positive and life-affirming action. Because depression often leads to feelings of hopeless and helplessness, it is important to create this counterweight to the inaction that depression can bring with it. CBT calls this behavioral activation (Tolin, 2016, p. 224).

What Should Be Included in a Safety Plan?

Use the OGS Safety Plan form to create your safety plan. This form will identify:

- Concerning thoughts

- Concerning behaviors

- Things the client can do (behavioral activation to shift attention)

- People the client can talk to (behavioral activation aimed at changing attentional focus to supportive and caring relationships)

- Triggers and removal of triggers from the environment. If medications are a trigger, they should be secured. No person with suicidal thoughts should have access to firearms in the home. Even if they are locked away, the risk of gaining access is there, and a plan should be made to temporarily remove any firearms from the home.

Can a Safety Plan Guarantee the Safety of Your Client?

A safety plan cannot guarantee the safety of your client, it does, however, indicate that you and your client have adequately addressed the issue of suicidal thoughts and behaviors and that you, the clinician, have actively taken all appropriate steps to help your client stay safe and alive.

What About Children?

When creating a safety plan with a child, the parent must always be involved. If a child discloses a safety issue and the parent is not present, you must contact the parent immediately (and notify your supervisor). A meeting must be scheduled on the same day to create a safety plan. Remember, safety planning is a collaborative process. A meaningful safety plan involves addressing both the concerns of the parent and the concerns of the child.

Here Is What Will Not Work:

- Meeting with the client and parent with a ready-made safety plan that does not take into account the specific family circumstances.

- Creating a vague safety plan including statements such as "will call a friend" or "parent will put away all medications."

- Things that are impossible such as "parent will supervise client at all times" when the parent works full-time.

Here Is What Will Work:

- Being compassionate toward and inquisitive about the client's and family's specific circumstances. Learn as much as you can to collaboratively create a workable safety plan.

- Being specific. Outline specifically where the client will go, who the client can call (include phone numbers), and what the client will do. An example of this would be: "Client will build a Lego Tower in the kitchen while guardian . . ."

- Listing things that are possible, such as: "Parent will ensure appropriate supervision of client. Aunt (insert aunt's name) will play Legos/go for a walk with client."

What If Nothing Works?

Sometimes nothing seems to work. When this is the case, it is important to consider the following factors:

- Is there anything reinforcing the client's need to be hospitalized? In other words, will the client receive more attention and perhaps compassion if he is so ill that he requires hospitalization? Is attention what the client actually needs? If so, how can your client receive more attention? Is a partial hospitalization program needed? Some form of respite? Keep in mind that your client may express an actual need— this is not manipulation on the client's part. Your client may not be able to tell you (yet) what he needs. This, in itself, is a clinical issue that requires attention.

- If your client is a child: Is the parent simply exhausted from caring for a mentally ill child? Is a more intensive level of service needed? Is respite needed? Does the parent need her own services?

- Is the client/family in a very dysregulated state? Can you assist with helping calm emotions? Can you instill hope that things will get better?

Sometimes hospitalization is needed to stabilize a very depressed client. This does not mean that you or the client missed something. It does mean that a better plan is needed. It is important to begin with planning for discharge right away. What will be different? What can you do? What can your client do? How can the environment change?

A Word About Suicide Risk and Persistent Depressive Disorder

What is Persistent Depressive Disorder?

This is diagnosed when clients have suffered from persistent low mood for at least 2 years (for children the time frame is 1 year), with or without any symptoms of a major depressive episode.

In the fifth edition of the *Diagnostic and Statistical Manual of Mental Disorders* (DSM-5; 2013) this combination of symptoms is called persistent depressive disorder (300.4).

What About Suicide Risk and Persistent Depressive Disorder?

If your client has suffered from persistent low mood and is now experiencing additional symptoms of major depression (including hopelessness), assess for suicide risk. Your client may feel that the additional heavy weight of major depression is just too much for her to handle. This can put her at a higher risk for suicidal thoughts and behaviors.

When your client has persistent depressive disorder that has always included or now includes symptoms of major depression, you must assess for suicide risk.

Safety always comes first. If there are client behaviors such as suicidal gestures or actions or severe self-harm (that may not be intended to lead to death, but could result in death), these need to be addressed first. There are many ways in which CBT responds to suicidal behaviors. Here are some of them:

- Make the environment safe by identifying and removing triggers from the environment.

- Change client behavioral responses to triggers.

- Increase skills to manage triggers and resulting emotional states (skill building).

- Examine and change automatic thoughts leading to suicidal behaviors.

Treatment Planning in CBT

Is it necessary to address all three elements of the cognitive triad in the treatment plan? What about behavioral interventions for those who struggle with thinking things through, which is common in depression?

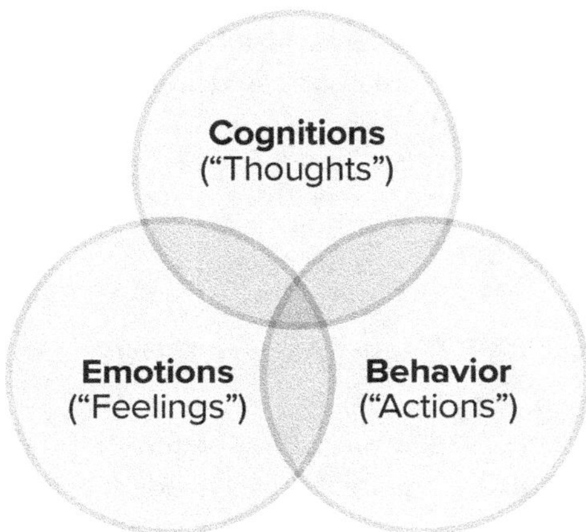

Figure 6. The cognitive triad.

It is not necessary to address all three elements of the cognitive triad equally and right away. In fact, Tolin (2016), referring to behavioral interventions, recommends that "you should strongly consider using these strategies as the 'main course' in your CBT" (p. 161).

Why start with behavioral interventions?

Generally speaking, interventions targeting behaviors may be more accessible to clients. In addition, when it comes to the treatment of depression, we are looking to move the client into action, as inaction is a part of the range of depressive symptoms.

In other words, targeting behavioral symptoms may be the most accessible "door" to treating depression. They make sense. When a client is socially isolated, creating a schedule of activities is a logical step. The client cannot think himself out of his isolation. But overcoming the isolation is likely to change his thinking and the way he feels about himself.

Community Mental Health Practice Alert

Therapy-interfering conditions can lead to skills deficits in people who are otherwise competent. Poverty may lead to an educational impairment. It is difficult to learn when you are hungry or worried about housing. It is difficult to learn when you have to move a lot. If you grew up in an old house and you have been exposed to lead, learning can become a real challenge.

While our clients may have skills deficits, this does not mean that they are incapable of learning. It is not a good idea to underestimate our clients' ability to learn, grow, and overcome.

Psychoeducation and behavioral interventions can be very empowering for our clients. The experience of competence is powerful and can lead to further changes in thinking, feeling, and behavior—just the kind of ripple effect we are looking for.

How to Build a CBT Treatment Plan:

1. Address safety issues first. This includes creating a safety plan right away if one is needed. If you are unsure if one is needed, consult with your supervisor.
2. Start with behavioral interventions such as creating a schedule of activities, building real-world skills, building relationships, and becoming active.
3. Address cognitive elements such as automatic thoughts as they occur. Help your client change negative automatic self-talk. If your client has had some success using behavioral interventions, this will be a natural step as you now have evidence that your client is learning to competently manage her life and that things can go well. Help your client use the evidence!
4. Address faulty thinking such as "things need to go well all the time."
5. Be on the lookout for core beliefs and use Socratic questioning to address faulty core beliefs.

What Are Socratic questions?

Tolin (2016) defines Socratic questions as "a way of helping the client arrive at a conclusion by asking carefully worded questions" (p. 159).

Here Are Some Examples of Socratic Questions:

- What does this mean to you?
- How did you come to think about the event this way?
- Is there another possible way of thinking about this event?
- How do you know that what you are thinking is true?

What Socratic Questioning Is Not:

- Getting the client to agree with you ("lip service"). Here is an example of lip service: "Don't you agree with that . . . ?" This is a yes/no question. It does not invite thinking and exploration.
- Manipulating the client to agree with you.
- Getting the client to think exactly like you.

What Socratic Questioning Is:

Socratic questioning is a process of asking open-ended questions that point your client in the direction of alternative and more realistic ways of thinking about a problem. Socratic questions point in the direction of evidence. It is up to your client to discover the answers to your Socratic questions and the impact that the newly discovered evidence can have on thinking, feelings, and being.

You may wonder: Can't I just tell my client what is wrong with the way he is thinking?

There is no real evidence that telling a client what to think and feel is effective. Just think about yourself: Most of us want a say. We feel that we are right and if we are not, it may take us some time to make adjustments to the way we think about something. We consider the evidence, sometimes reluctantly. And we adjust our thinking because we are in conversation with someone who cares about us. Our clients are no different. They make changes to their ways of thinking and doing things because they discover new meanings and interpretations in conversation with us.

The Golden Rule of CBT

Listen compassionately. Then ask questions that point your client in the direction of evidence that can change the way he thinks, feels, and behaves.

Heather's Treatment Plan

Heather's treatment plan will need to address the following problems as identified in her Diagnostic Evaluation and case conceptualization:

Cognitive: Attention focused on hopelessness, hence thoughts of suicide as escape, must address first/possible safety issue.

Behavioral: Basic self-care is lacking—poor nutrition, sleeping too much, poor hygiene, not taking care of fundamentals (may become homeless), lack of interaction with her children.

Emotional: Sadness, hopelessness, shame.

Once again, working collaboratively is paramount. If identification of goals is a problem, ask the miracle question (Jong & Berg, 2013): *If you had one wish and it would come true tomorrow morning, what would your wish be?* Build collaboration based on that wish.

In Heather's case, you would already have identified safety issues as a problem and would have already created a safety plan. Elimination of suicidal behaviors and reduction of suicidal thoughts and feelings of hopelessness are crucial to Heather's treatment plan.

Heather's most important goal for the time being, then, may look like this:

Goal 1: Heather will reduce/eliminate suicidal thoughts/behaviors.

Method 1: Heather will develop and follow a safety plan and/or crisis management plan to manage escalation of symptoms.

How are you going to know that Heather is following her plan and getting better?

You and Heather are going to review the plan at every session and revise it as needed. Your review together should collect data every time. How many times on average did Heather think about suicide during the course of the day? You may want to develop a checklist attached to her safety plan. Did she follow her safety plan? What made things better, what made things worse? Use the data you collect for ongoing revision of her safety plan.

Method 2: Heather will identify triggers for suicidal thoughts and behaviors, and develop more adaptive ways of responding to triggers.

Here is where you and Heather can talk about automatic thoughts and perhaps core beliefs (when the time is right). If triggers are environmental, you can make a plan to remove as many as possible.

Goal 2: Heather will increase positive social interactions.

Method 1: Heather will connect with family and friends on a daily basis.

You may want to develop a menu of activities that Heather is willing to engage in, and then monitor if Heather is actually engaging in those activities.

Goal 3: Heather will develop a sense of hope and purpose.

Method 1: Heather will identify and reduce negative automatic thoughts.

Method 2: Heather will increase more realistic thoughts about self, others, and the world.

Method 3: Heather will engage in a meaningful activity at least once a day.

Note that everything in Heather's treatment plan serves the purpose of helping her decrease her symptoms of depression.

It starts with safety, then moves to behavioral activation (increasing social interactions), and finally addresses Heather's thinking.

Note that you can begin treatment with just Goal 1. A treatment plan is a work in progress and should be adjusted as necessary. Ongoing collaboration is the key to successful treatment planning and successful treatment. Work on the treatment plan with the client. Say things like: *This is your plan. Is there anything on your plan that we should change? What is working for you? What is not working?*

What Is the Role of the Therapeutic Relationship in CBT?

Beck (1979) clearly states that attention must be paid to the therapeutic relationship. CBT is more than a set of techniques (p. 27). Dobson and Dobson (2017) compare the therapeutic relationship to the "vehicle" that drives change (p. 67). Tolin (2016) references Carl Rogers in calling for empathy, genuineness, and unconditional positive regard (p. 11).

But Tolin (2016) also makes it clear "that the therapeutic relationship is *necessary*, but not *sufficient*" (p. 138).

CBT is focused on what is happening here and now. In order to help your client, you have to attend to what is happening here and now. You have to attend to the therapeutic relationship, because the relationship drives the change process. If something is wrong in the relationship between the therapist and the client—the relationship is not collaborative and the client does not trust the therapist—then change is unlikely.

Here is a visual representation of the role of the therapeutic relationship in CBT:

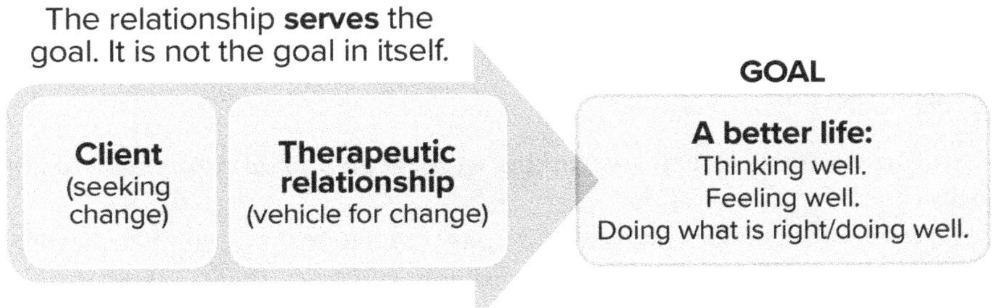

Figure 7

Being Attuned: Building Affect Regulation in the Therapeutic Relationship

Being attuned to your client's emotional state is just as important in CBT as it is in any other form of therapy. Attunement builds the therapeutic relationship.

If your client feels and knows that you are attuned with him, then he is much more likely to trust you. But attunement is not enough in CBT.

Let's take a look at the cognitive triad again:

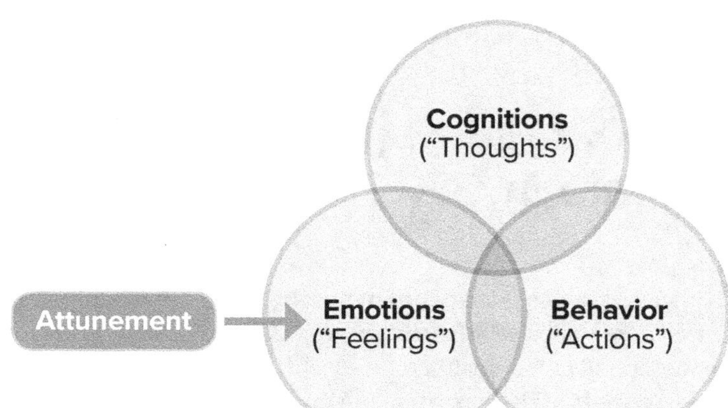

Figure 8

Attunement puts you in touch with your client's emotional state. It gives you an idea how your client feels. You can then better assess what drives her behavior.
You can adjust:

- How you are with your client: You can lower your voice if your client seems agitated and feels threatened, but is still unaware of this. You can move your body further away to reduce client feelings of panic or fear.

- What you do with your client: You can offer a blanket or turn on soft music to increase client feelings of safety.

- What you say to your client: You can ask your client if she is feeling threatened/lonely/desperate.

When you are attuning, you are working with the emotional component of the cognitive triad.
Attunement by itself does not "fix" anything, but it helps your client feel more comfortable. If your client feels more comfortable and trusts that you are attuned with her and can handle the complex and intense emotions she is feeling, then she is much more likely to be able to move into action.
In other words: If you are attuned with your client, she may be more willing and able to move into work within the cognitive and behavioral component of the cognitive triad. Attunement is an important part of the therapeutic relationship.

What About Co-regulation?

Co-regulation is a term coined by the Allan Schore (Schore, 2008; Schore & Schore, 2016), the founder of modern attachment theory. Co-regulation is not a CBT term or technique, but understanding co-regulation can be helpful when using CBT.

Co-regulation happens when you, the provider, attune with your client. This attunement is initially a right-brain-to-right-brain process, meaning that it happens naturally. Once you are attuned with your client, once you sense that your client is emotionally dysregulated and may need help with affect regulation, you can help your client regulate.

Co-regulation is not a verbal process, but it involves a decision on your part, namely to help your client regulate. You may want to breathe slower, relax your body, shift your gaze, or change the tone of your voice. Your state of mind and body can have an impact of your client's state of mind and body. You can help your client down-regulate an intense affective state using co-regulation.

Co-regulatory processes happen in therapeutic and other relationships all the time. You may want to use co-regulation when your client is not ready or able to consciously, verbally work on the regulation of intense affective states—perhaps because no one has modeled this effectively for him.

How does co-regulation fit into the cognitive triad of CBT?

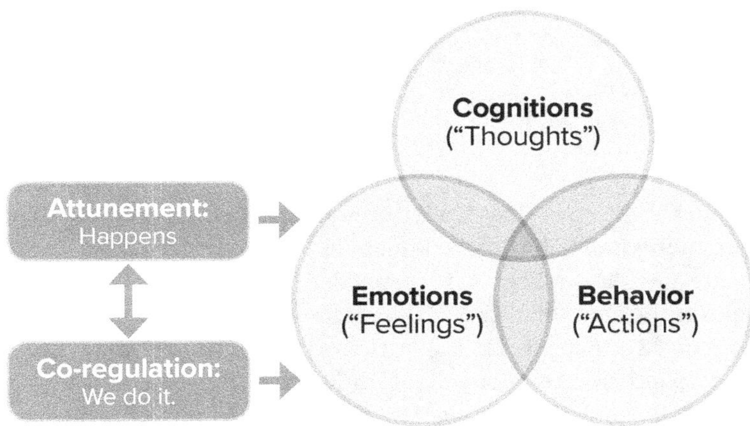

Figure 9

Co-regulation may be needed when your client is "stuck" in an unregulated and intense affective state and unable to reflect on his emotions.

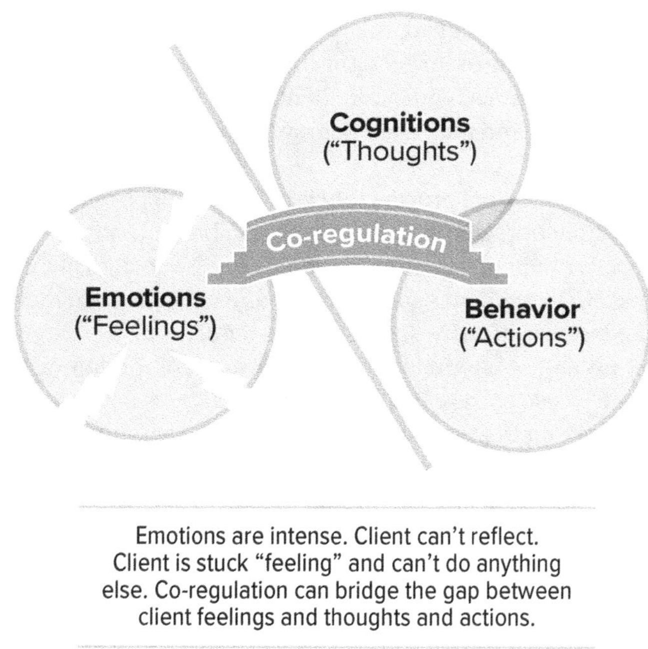

Emotions are intense. Client can't reflect. Client is stuck "feeling" and can't do anything else. Co-regulation can bridge the gap between client feelings and thoughts and actions.

Figure 10

Co-regulation builds the bridge from the emotional component of the cognitive triad to the cognitive and behavioral components. When your client is stuck in an emotional state, unable to reflect on it, co-regulation helps your client build a connection; it moves the emotional part of the cognitive triad back into the triad. You can now focus on CBT instead of being stuck working on feelings only. You could also say that co-regulation gets your client ready to do CBT.

Ultimately the experience of co-regulation is meant to implicitly teach self-regulation. If your client already self-regulates well, co-regulation is not really needed. Attunement, however, will and should continue.

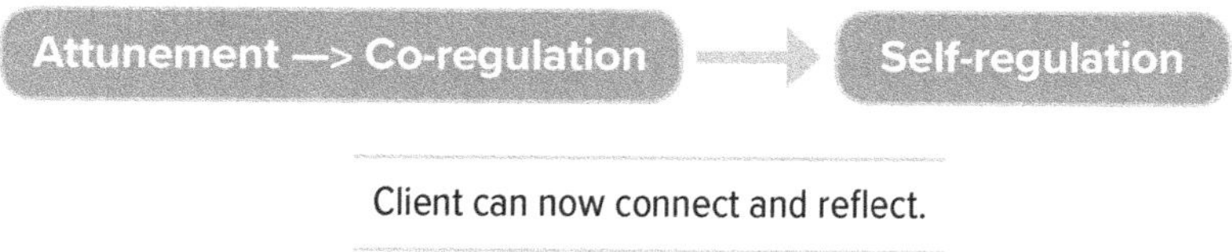

Client can now connect and reflect.

Figure 11

Just like attunement, co-regulation is used in the service of accessing the full cognitive triad with your client. When you are doing CBT, co-regulation is not enough; it is a means, a vehicle for change.

A Word on Co-regulation and Depressive States of Mind

Before you can help a client regulate a depressive, perhaps even suicidal state of mind using co-regulation, you have to be willing and able to attune to the client's depressive state. You have to be able to feel with and for him what he is going through. Feeling someone else's despair and hopelessness is no easy task. The key is to feel with the client, to be with the client, but not to make his state of mind and feelings your own.

You are not taking on the client's depression, but you are getting to know it, so that you can then help him regulate. If you are attuned with your client and you are helping him co-regulate, he is no longer alone. This, in itself, can help lift the intense feelings of loneliness and despair.

CBT Techniques and CBT Structure

Sometimes CBT can seem a bit formulaic to a therapist. This can happen when you think of CBT as a set of rules and techniques. You may think that you have to use an automatic thought record if you are doing CBT with a client. Or you may rigidly stick to an established structure for a session, when what is needed is some flexibility and attunement with your client.

Tolin (2016) uses the analogy of being a chef verses being a cook (p. 9).

When you are doing CBT: Be a chef. Add your own flavor. Serve what the client is likely going to eat. But also serve something that stretches the client's palate. This is how your client grows.

Keep in mind that you can use many kinds of techniques when doing CBT, as long as this is done within the context of the foundation of CBT and you are working with your client on changing cognitions, emotions, and behavior.

Still, there are ways in which CBT is different from other forms of therapy. CBT is more directive and more structured than other forms of treatment for depression (such as interpersonal psychotherapy). Treatment has a structure. There are things to be learned. Every session has a structure. You can step away from the structure of the session. You can be flexible when necessary. But when you are doing so, you are very much aware that you are doing this and why you are doing this. To stick with the culinary analogy: There is a menu. The menu can vary, but there is always a menu. For the treatment of depression this makes sense: Depression can make your clients feel aimless. They may have no structure in their days and no plan for how to move forward.

CBT creates a structure and a plan for your client. The message to your client is: There is a way out of your depression. I can teach you the steps you need to take.

Creating Structure

Treatment has a structure: As Tolin (2016) puts it: "CBT tends to not be a forever, Woody Allen-style treatment" (p. 8).

Treatment is focused on the collaboratively established goals, not on other things that come up in the course of treatment or the course of a session. This does not mean that treatment goals can't be revised if this is needed. If a client develops suicidal ideation while in treatment, clearly the treatment plan needs to be revisited and revised.

As client problems vary, so does length of treatment. Dobson and Dobson (2017) reference a 12- to 16-session length. But this length refers to length of treatment in treatment studies.

Community Mental Health Practice Alert

Clients in a community mental health setting often present with a multiplicity of symptoms and problems. Our clients are often dually diagnosed. And they are often also physically ill. They may have depression and PTSD. They may have lifelong exposure to toxic stress.

At OhioGuidestone, more than 55% of our clients may have an ACE score of 4 or more, putting them at a much higher risk for a variety of physical and mental health problems. (The ACE score is a measure of adverse childhood experiences obtainable at the Aces Too High website, www.acestoohigh.com.) What this means is that your client may have depression and diabetes or depression and heart disease. She may also struggle with an addiction that is diagnosed or undiagnosed.

What does this mean for treatment duration?

If your client struggles with more than one mental health problem and additional physical and environmental problems, it is unlikely that treatment duration will fall within the 12- to 16-week range.

It is important, however, to keep in mind and to discuss with your client that treatment has a course: There is a beginning and an end. The goal of treatment is to resolve the mental health issues that brought your client into treatment. Both you and your client should be aware where you are in the treatment. Are you just beginning? Are you in the midst of it? Or are you almost done? You and your client should frequently discuss this.

Once again, creating structure is important. If your client feels that she has so many problems she may never be done with treatment, this could contribute to a sense of hopelessness. When using CBT, length of treatment can vary depending on the complexity of symptoms and problems. Structure, however, is a constant.

Creating Structure When Discussing Course and Length of Treatment

You can use a simple visual aid like this to discuss the course of treatment and possible length of treatment with your client.

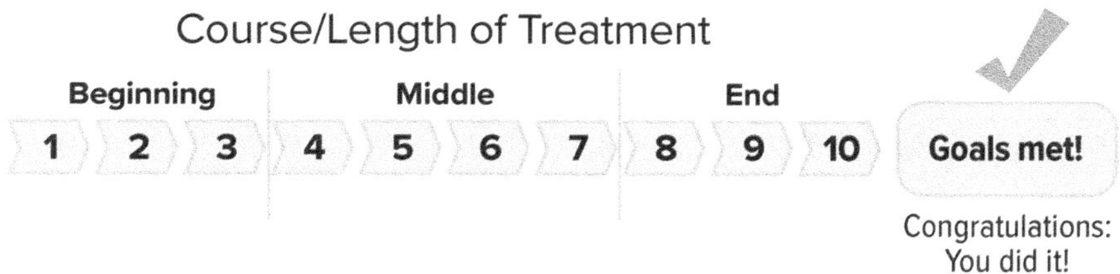

Figure 12

Creating Structure for Each Session

Here is an example of how you can structure a session with your client:

CBT Session Structure

1. **Check-in:** This is brief, perhaps 5 minutes. Is there anything new that is relevant to treatment? Has the client's depression gotten better, worse, or remained the same?
2. **Identify today's tasks:** Again, this is brief. Identify what needs to be done today. Be collaborative about this. If your client is unfocused and wants to add things that are not relevant to treatment, it is OK to be directive and refer to treatment goals. If new things have come up, help the client evaluate how they fit into treatment and rate how important it is to address them right now. Will they detour treatment or will they move the client forward?
3. **Homework review:** Homework is an integral component of CBT. Homework brings the content of therapy into the real world. This is where skills will need to be practiced and new ways of thinking/doing/feeling be tried. Celebrate successes, even the small ones, and problem-solve about things that did not work.
4. **Work on today's tasks:** This is the "meat" of your session. Be sure to anchor your work in the treatment plan and the cognitive triad. This is where your behavioral, emotional, or cognitive work takes place.
5. **Summarize the work:** You are the "guide" through treatment and through each session. Summarize periodically what you are talking about and how this fits into treatment progress.
6. **Assign homework:** New homework can originate from the homework review at the beginning of the session and/or today's tasks. You and the client can identify what needs practice. Be sure that homework can realistically be accomplished.
7. **Closing:** Summarizing session takeaways. Clarification of questions. Feedback about session.

Adapted from Persons, Davidson, and Tompkins, Essential Components of Cognitive-Behavior Therapy for Depression, APA, Washington, DC, 2001 (p. 59).

Here is a simplified version to keep handy for your client as you travel through each session is available in the appendix.

CBT Session Structure
Check-In
Identify Today's Task
Homework Review
Work on Today's Task
Summarize the Work
Identify New Homework
Closing

Essential CBT Techniques

Remember, CBT can borrow techniques from a variety of evidence-based forms of therapy such as Dialectical Behavior Therapy or Acceptance and Commitment Therapy. There are, however, a few essential intervention components you should use.

Psychoeducation

Dobson and Dobson (2017) define psychoeducation as "the provision of information about relevant psychological principles and knowledge" (p. 96).

Psychoeducation takes place throughout the course of treatment. At the beginning of treatment, you should provide client-appropriate information about the following:

- Symptoms and treatment of depression.

- CBT. (You can think of this as CBT 101). Go over the cognitive triad (but don't call it that). It is important that your client understands that he will be working on thoughts, feelings, and behaviors and that these are connected. You can also determine together where the client is most willing and able to start work. For many of our clients, behavioral work is the most accessible. Explain that CBT is collaborative, structured, focused, and present oriented.

- Resources. Periodically assess what your client needs. Does he need access to an advocacy or support group? Legal assistance? Job training? Resource building is an important aspect of CBT because increased access to resources gives your client an opportunity to act. As depression can lead to complete helplessness and inaction, helping your client build a road map for action can be life changing.

Socratic Questioning

Socratic questioning is a process of asking open ended questions that point your client in the direction of alternative and more realistic ways of thinking about a problem. Socratic questions point in the direction of evidence. It is up to your client to discover the answers to your Socratic questions and the impact that the newly discovered evidence can have on thinking, feelings, and acting. Remember, telling your client the answers to the questions you are asking is not effective. In CBT you should be asking a lot of Socratic questions. As tempting as it may be to give your client answers, they would be your answers, not his.

Homework

Tolin (2016) identifies the following five kinds of homework (p. 154):

1. Reading Assignments

Reading assignments are tailored to the client's specific needs and abilities.

This can be tricky for our clients. Keep in mind that many of our adult clients read on a third-grade level. Assess your client's ability to take in written information. Keep it simple. Use handouts that contain visual representations of the information you want your client to review. Reading assignments are, of course, a form of psychoeducation. They are also designed to empower and change the way your client thinks about himself, others, and the world.

2. Self-Monitoring

You can create simple checklists to help your client monitor problematic behaviors and thoughts. Be sure to explain that self-monitoring is designed to establish baseline and determine treatment needs. Here is what a simple monitoring chart could look like:

	Mon	Tue	Wed	Thu	Fri	Sat	Sun
Hours in bed							
Hours of TV							

Figure 13

You can use this chart over the course of several weeks to monitor decreased time spent in bed, if this is a goal. Honesty, of course, is key to self-monitoring. Be sure that you collaborate with your client on a realistic goal and a charting system that feels right for him.

3. Learning and Practicing New Behaviors

Skills Training

New skills will have to be learned together in session, then practiced in the real world. In other words: It is easier to talk about a new skill/new behavior than to engage in the new skill/behavior. You should explain to your client that there is no such thing as failure when practicing a new skill or behavior. Each "mistake" is a learning opportunity, guiding both of you to make changes, refine the work, and examine negative automatic thoughts.

Behavior Changes

Your depressed client may need specific behavior changes. You may want to assign a specific behavior that you want your client to increase. It is a good idea to use a self-monitoring chart to track the new behavior. Be sure to keep it simple and set realistic goals. Instead of asking your client to visit a family member or friend every day, suggest 3 out of 7 days. Then identify specifically who your client will contact and make sure that your client has a valid phone number or address. Here is a simple chart to monitor behavior change:

	Mon	Tue	Wed	Thu	Fri	Sat	Sun
Contacted friend/family member X							

Figure 14

By setting a realistic goal, you are making sure your client can be successful now. This is especially important when your client is very depressed. Celebrate the small successes, then raise the bar. For example, move from the task of contacting a person to the task of spending time with that person.

What if my client has no family or friends? Continue to keep in mind how important collaboration is. Know your client! If your client is really and truly completely isolated and has no one in the world to support her, this is an important clinical issue by itself. Go back to resource building. Brainstorm with your client. Find a support or advocacy group. Connect your client with peer supports. All of this creates a path to action.

4. Behavioral Activation

Because depression comes with a loss of pleasure in formerly pleasurable activities, many clients become inactive when depressed. This makes sense, at least on the surface. Why would anyone engage in an activity that gives no pleasure? A vicious cycle of inactivity ensues:

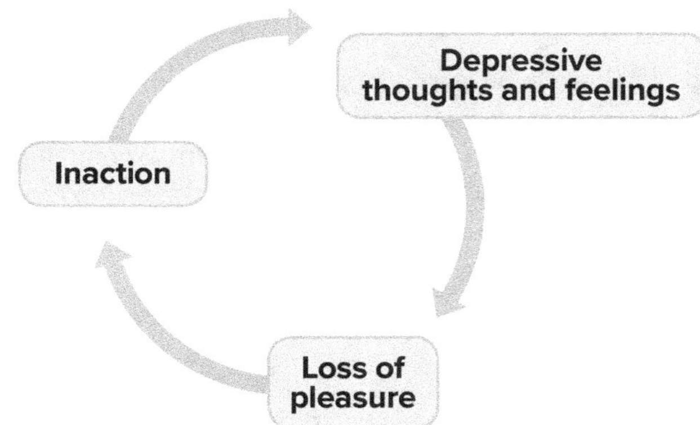

Figure 15

Provide psychoeducation to your client about this cycle. Explain that if you change just one part of the cycle, the whole cycle can begin to change. Say you understand that changing depressive thoughts and feelings can be hard and suggest that the client start by changing behaviors—scheduling activities and altering the environment (going new places and seeing new people). Explain that it is OK if activities are not "fun" at first, that this is simply a symptom of depression. Explain that over time and with practice, enjoyment will return.

Here is what the cycle of behavioral change will look like:

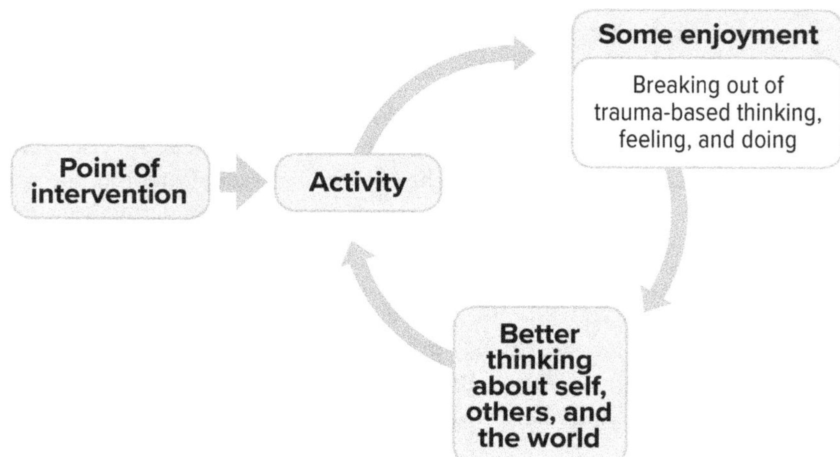

Figure 16

Tolin (2016) outlines the benefits of activity scheduling and explains that it goes hand in hand with self-monitoring. While it is good to be ambitious about behavioral changes and activity scheduling, it is equally important to be realistic about it.

You are teaching your client to create achievable and realistic behavioral goals (pp. 224–226).

Here is a simple Activity Schedule you can use with clients. The further you are in treatment, the more meaningful activities you may want to schedule.

	Mon	Tue	Wed	Thu	Fri	Sat	Sun
Morning							
Afternoon							
Evening							

Figure 17

5. Cognitive Restructuring

Let's take another look at the role of thoughts/cognitions in CBT.

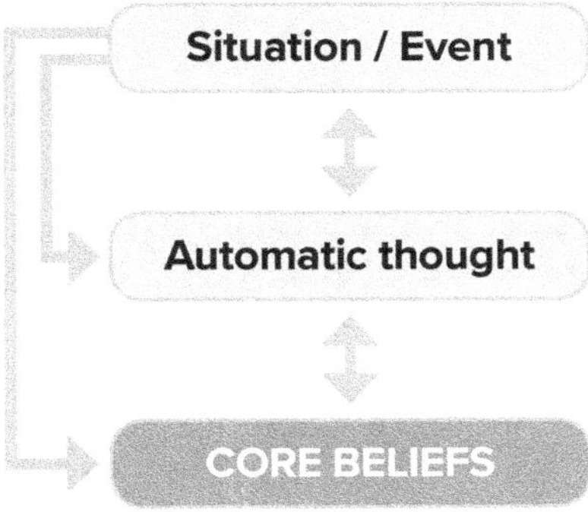

Figure 18: Note that core beliefs are much harder to identify than automatic thoughts. Automatic thoughts just appear; we do not have to ask for them. Because they appear so often, they are easier to bring into conscious awareness.

Negative and faulty core beliefs are at the root of depressive thoughts and feelings. But those core beliefs can be difficult to uncover. Core beliefs are triggered by a situation or event. Once a core belief is triggered, it sends out its "messengers"—those pesky negative automatic thoughts.

Negative automatic thoughts are much easier to address, because they show up all the time and may even "bug" your client.

Here are some examples of automatic thoughts:

- I always mess everything up.

- She hates me.

- I am going to fail this one.

Automatic thoughts can be examined. In CBT, you and your client are looking for evidence for and against the truth of the automatic thought.

Here is what this would look like:

A situation or event triggers a negative automatic thought, which in turn will negatively affect the way your client feels. But what if the thought was just a thought? Like the brain letting off some steam? Then we should be able to examine thoughts and ask: Is this a realistic thought? Or is this just my brain blowing off some steam (You could use the term *brain fart*.)

Automatic Thought (AT)	Evidence for AT	Evidence Against AT
I mess everything up.	I lost my phone.	<ul><li>I went to work today.</li><li>I found my phone.</li><li>My sister called me to ask for advice.</li><li>. . .</li></ul>
She hates me.	She is mad at me about the thing I said.	<ul><li>We have been dating for 6 months.</li><li>We make each other laugh.</li><li>She called me to talk.</li><li>. . .</li></ul>
I am failing.	Failed spelling test.	<ul><li>Just got into district art show.</li><li>Passing grades, even in spelling.</li><li>. . .</li></ul>

Figure 19

Here is a blank version for you to use with your clients:

Automatic Thought (AT)	Evidence for AT	Evidence Against AT

Figure 20

Keep in mind that automatic thoughts can be relentless. Once you have examined them with your client, it is OK to use humor when one shows up. You can talk to an automatic thought! Here is an example:

> "Hello, there. There you are again trying to trick me. Not going to happen. You, my uninvited friend, are just a brain fart, stinky and unpleasant. I am going to leave you now and think better thoughts. Good-bye!"

Talking to the automatic thought in this manner creates distance from it. It is far easier to examine a faulty thought from a distance. If your client can dismiss those faulty automatic thoughts, then he can begin to let go of the feelings based on those thoughts.

If you and your client run into a set of automatic thoughts with a similar theme, you are probably on to a core belief. Core beliefs, too, can be examined for their truthfulness.

CBT Interventions for Depression

Interventions Targeting the Behavioral Component of the Cognitive Triad

Interventions targeting the behavioral components contributing to depressive symptoms are often your first step. Keep in mind that the components of the cognitive triad overlap. When you are working with your client to change behaviors, automatic thoughts may come up in conversation. This is a natural opportunity to begin psychoeducation about the cognitive triad and cognitive components of depression.

It is, however, important to stay on task. If you and your client have collaboratively agreed to work on behaviors for the session, this is what you should do. Sometimes talking about cognitions can lead to insight and behavioral change. Sometimes talking about cognitions can be a distraction, a way to avoid having to plan for and create behavioral changes.

The following interventions are meant to begin after the diagnostic evaluation and initial treatment plan have been completed.

Images you will need are included in the intervention description. Feel free to print them for your client as needed. Here are some other things you will need for many interventions: paper, index cards, writing tools for all ages, coloring pencils, markers, scissors, tape.

INTERVENTION 1

Building the House of CBT

Your first session will likely center around building a collaborative relationship with your client and educating her about CBT. Because CBT lives in the house of a caring and collaborative relationship, relationship building and monitoring will be ongoing throughout treatment. Because your client may not have been exposed to CBT, there is a strong educational component in your first session.

Note that because your client is depressed, initially, relationship building will be your responsibility. In other words, you will be doing a lot of modeling. You will model and embody caring and compassion. The caring and compassionate relationship with your client is the vehicle for change.

Target skill: Understanding the roles of thoughts, feelings, and behaviors in symptom development and symptom reduction.

1. Ask your client how she is and what brought her to treatment. Listen and respond with compassion. Here are some things you could say or ask. Be sure to take notes when your client talks about her experience of depression:

   - *It sounds like your depression is telling you that you can't do anything right, that nothing is worth anything.*

   - *It sounds like everything seems too hard right now, even getting out of bed and taking a shower.*

   - *This must be hard for you.*

   - *I wonder about your life before depression. Can you tell me about what you used to do/used to like?*

   - *What has depression taken away from you?*

   - *What would you like to get back?*

2. Identify today's task: learning to work with CBT to decrease depressive symptoms. Use a picture of the cognitive triad to very briefly explain how CBT works.

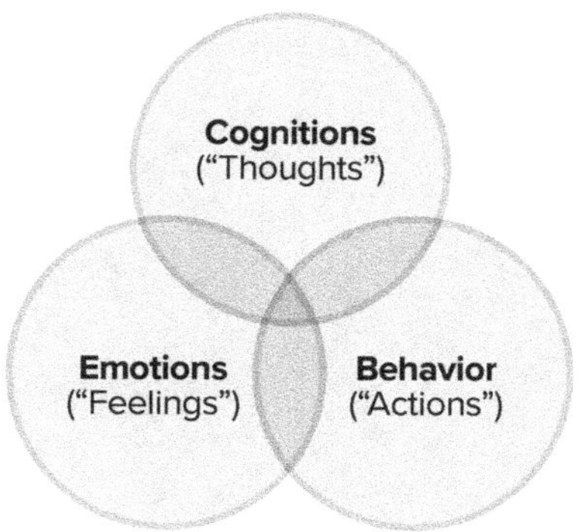

Figure 21

Keep this explanation short. Because your client is depressed, her cognitive processes are likely slowed and she can't take in too much information.

Here are some things you could say:

- *You know, the ways we think, feel, and do things are connected.*

- *Not everything we think is helpful. Which of your thoughts are not helpful to you?*

- *Not everything we think is true.*

- *Sometimes our thinking gets us stuck.*

- *Sometimes the way we think does not fit the situation we are in.*

- *Sometimes our feelings match what is going on in our lives, sometimes they do not. Just like thoughts, feelings can be a good fit for a situation or not. When our thoughts and feelings "run away" from what is really happening, what we do can also be a mismatch to what is needed.*

3. Work on today's task: go back to your client's answers about what depression has taken away from her and what she would like back. Here is a simple chart you could use:

What depression has taken away from me:	What I would like back:

Figure 22

4. Complete this form with your client. Your client can write in the form, but if she is not ready to, you can be her scribe. If your client agrees to write on the form, compliment her on taking action.

5. Once the form is completed, discuss with your client what she wants back. Elicit details. Perhaps she once had friends and depression took those friends from her. What did she do with them? What kinds of feelings did she have when spending time with her friends? When asking these ques-

tions, you are implicitly teaching your client about the relationship between behaviors and feelings.

6. Explore ways in which depression is a thief. Explain that you and she together can catch the thief, unmask him, and throw him out of the house. What is a thief going to do? Well, he will try to come back, of course! Then you have to unmask him and throw him out again.

7. Explore ways in which depression is a con man. A con man will tell you any-thing. Depression will try to con you into thinking that there is no other way. Depression will con you into not leaving the house. Depression will con you into thinking that nothing you do matters. And what will a con man do if you don't believe him? He will tell you another lie, a bigger one. Perhaps depres-sion is trying to con you into believing that your life is meaningless, that you should not even be alive?

8. Summarize today's work: You have explored what depression has taken from your client and what she would like back. You have explored the ways in which depression tries to con your client into faulty beliefs.

9. Now, identify homework with your client. In this case, you may want to give your client a printout of today's chart and have her create a more extended list of what depression has taken away from her and what she wants back.

10. Additionally, send your client home with a note card outlining the new way of thinking about depression:

    Never believe a con man.

    Never trust a thief.

    Depression is a con man and a thief.

    Ask her to read this note card at the beginning and the end of every day.

11. Finally, get feedback from your client. How did today's session go? What was helpful? Is there anything she did not understand? If your client is worried about not understanding the cognitive triad, reassure her that things will become clear as time goes by.

INTERVENTION 2

Diving into Doing: Taking Stock

When people have been depressed for a long period of time, they often lose track of how time is spent. It becomes normal to spend a lot of time watching television or playing video games. This intervention is designed to help your client begin to notice how much time is spent in depression-maintaining activities.

Target skill: Insight about depression-maintaining activities.

1. Begin with your check-in. This also means beginning with empathy. Ask your client how he has been feeling and how he is feeling today. Use language that implies that thoughts and feelings are important, but not always true.

    Here is an example of what this may sound like:

    - *What have your thoughts been telling you this week?*

    - *How about your feelings? What have they been telling you?*

2. Identify today's task: taking stock of how your client spends time. Collaboratively explore what might be on the CBT menu today. Explain that it is often important to establish what is actually happening outside the therapy setting. Wonder out loud what your client is doing in the course of his day.

3. Review the homework together: Take a look at what your client has added to last week's chart ("What depression has taken from me/What I would like back"). Again, ask your client to specify what he would like back. Paint a detailed picture that evokes the emotion of the activity/situation your client would like back. In other words, help your client connect with a positive feeling about a past event/situation and bring it into the present.

4. You may have to pan for gold here. Many depressed clients struggle with recalling anything positive. Be a detective:, there is always a positive memory, moment, situation, or event your client can recall.

5. Work on today's task: Explain that you will take a look together at how your client is spending his time. Be sure to explain that this is not meant to make him feel upset about wasting time, but rather to take a look at what is happening right now. Show your client the following chart (the chart should only go up to the time of your current appointment):

Things I have done today:
7 AM–11 AM
11 AM–1 PM
1 PM–3 PM
3 PM–5 PM
5 PM–7 PM
7 PM–10 PM
After 10 PM

Figure 23

Help your client complete this chart. Once again, you may have to be your client's scribe. Explain the important of honesty. This is not yet about scheduling new activities—right now you are teaching your client about activity monitoring. If you are working with a child, the child can draw her activities.

6. Help your client look at patterns in what he is doing. It is easy to spend a lot of time in bed when suffering from depression, to watch a lot of TV or play a lot of video games. Explain to your client that inaction is a symptom of depression, not a personal fault.

7. Go back to the chart of what your client wants back in his life. Ask Socratic questions about how your client could get any one of those things back. Here is what this might sound like:

    - *Tell me more about going bowling with your friends. What was it like?*

    - *What kinds of feelings did you have when you went bowling with your friends?*

    - *How often did you go bowling with your friends?*

8. Summarize what you have done so far: You have taken a look at what your client has done today (activity monitoring) and at the things your client has been missing in his life due to depression.

9. Assign homework: Activity monitoring

10. Give your client three blank copies of today's chart. Ask him to complete the chart for 3 days.

11. Be specific. Explain that he should complete the chart as he is doing things, as it is often difficult to remember things even an hour later. Explain that the completed charts will help you and him see how he spends his day and that this will serve as a guide for building a path out of depression. Encourage your client to be honest. You are scientists together. If your client spends most of his time in bed, he should simply put this on his chart. Be sure to ask your client if he has any questions about today's session or the homework assignment.

12. What if this is all too complicated for my client?

    Simplify: You can ask your client what he does for most of the day. Your chart would look like this:

Most of the day I did these three things:
1
2.
3.

Figure 24

If you are working with a young child or with an adult who struggles with reading/writing, ask her to draw the items. You can then ask questions to specify what your client means. You want to be sure that you understand what your client is telling you.

13. Closing. Send your client home with words of encouragement. You can say things like:

    - *Taking stock in a great first step.*

    - *This will help you move toward the life you want.*

    - *Be kind to yourself. Depression may try to shame you about how you spend time. No need to listen.*

INTERVENTION 3

Diving into Doing: Activity Scheduling

There is an inherent danger in overdoing the scheduling of activities. It is not really normal or desirable to schedule have every minute of the day. There should always be some unstructured time. Overscheduling your depressed client will only lead to treatment failure or your client dropping out of treatment.

Target skill: Setting behavioral goals. Insight about the benefits of engaging in meaningful activities.

1. Check in with your client. Begin with empathy. Ask your client how she is today and how her week has been. Briefly assess her level of depression. At this point you should know your client a bit better and you should be able to read some of her nonverbal cues. Ask open-ended questions that help your client open up to you.

2. Collaboratively work with your client on establishing today's tasks. Discuss the purpose of activity monitoring (taking stock) and suggest that it is time to move on to activity scheduling. Emphasize that trying new things and reconnecting with old, meaningful things will make a difference.

3. Homework review: Take a look at your client's activity monitoring charts together. Whatever the charts are showing will be your baseline. Be sure to show empathy about the way your client is currently living her life. Depression conned her into inactivity. Inactivity feels right when you are depressed. The trouble is that it just perpetuates depression. Additionally, highlight any meaningful activities. You can say things like this:

   - *I see that you are already _______. That's amazing.*

   - *Part of you already does not believe the lies depression tells you. You are already _______.*

4. Work on today's task: Go back to some of the things your client is missing, the things depression has taken from her. How could your client get back to those things one step at a time? Here is a simple graph to help a client understand the purpose of activity scheduling:

Figure 25

5. If necessary, help your client understand that even when she is well, there will be periods of sadness and some periods of depression. This is part of being human. The question your client can ask herself should be: How is what I am doing helping me recover from depression and moving me toward the life I want?

6. Determine together what small steps your client can take during the next week to move toward a life worth living. Keep it simple. Perhaps your client used to go bowling with friends but has lost contact with them. Here are some activities your client could realistically schedule:

    - Look for your old address book. Find the phone number for at least one old friend.
    - Call that friend and leave a message.

    What if your client never had any friends? Can't remember having friends?

    Here are some realistic schedule items for her:

    - Find local support group.
    - Find local activity group.
    - Place one call to support/activity group.
    - Make plan to attend one meeting.
    - Select meeting.
    - Schedule meeting.
    - Attend meeting.

7. As you can see, you want to break down things into small steps that lead to your client's success. The last thing she needs is to feel like a failure in therapy.

8. Create a simple activity schedule with your client for the next week. Here is an example of what this may look like:

	Morning	**Afternoon**	**Evening**
Mon	Look for Joe's number for 10 minutes	Call Joe	Look online for support group
Tue			
Wed			
Thu			
Fri			

	Morning	Afternoon	Evening
Sat			
Sun			

Figure 26

Be realistic about scheduling. If your client currently does not get out of bed until 11 a.m., do not schedule an activity at 9 a.m. Collaborate with your client about the types of activities she will engage in. If your client tells you clearly that she will not engage in a specific activity, do not put that activity on her schedule yet. Choose an activity that is a challenge for your client, but not overwhelming. If your client is entirely inactive, just calling someone can be a big step. If you are working with a child, activities can be drawn instead of written out. Just make sure that the image clearly represents the activity. You can also serve as a scribe for the child.

9. Explain to your client what success means. In this case, success means that your client engaged in the scheduled activity. If she looked for the phone number, this is success. If she called her friend and left a message, this is success. Break seemingly insurmountable tasks down into small, manageable steps, then praise her for taking them. Update your activity schedule every session to include another step your client will take toward the final goal, like meeting an old (or new) friend, and eventually to living an active life.

10. Summarize with and for your client what you have done together: You have identified activities that move her in the direction of being an active agent in her life.

11. Identify new homework: In this case, the new homework is to complete the activities included in the activity chart. For some clients this may mean scheduling one new activity per day; for another client it may mean scheduling three. In subsequent sessions you will refine the chart, add to it, and delete what does not work. Be sure to always send a copy of the chart home with your client as a reminder and ask her to post it in a prominent place.

12. Don't forget to ask your client if she has any questions. Ask what worked well today.

13. What if your client complains that she is not enjoying any of this? Ask her to hang in there. Use your relational skills. Suggest that enjoyment will come with time. Not enjoying things is a symptom of depression. Enjoyment has to be relearned. Ask your client to try these activities for a while. Once you find the right ones, enjoyment will follow.

14. What if this is too complex for your client? Once again, simplify. Here is an example of how you could do so:

Activity Schedule for:	
Time:	

In this case you would give your client one piece of paper per day. You would schedule only one activity, to be completed either in the morning, afternoon, or evening. If your client cannot read well, simply have her draw the activity or draw it for her. Children may enjoy cutting out an image of the activity and gluing it into the activity schedule. Staple the daily sheets together for easy safekeeping. This increases your chance of getting them back for the next session.

15. Closing. Send your client home with words of encouragement like these:

   - *You can learn to do things simply by doing them.*

   - *Think of yourself as an explorer. You are venturing into new territory. This is exciting!*

INTERVENTION 4

Less of This: Activity Scheduling in Reverse

So far you have been trying to get your client to do more of the things that move him in the direction of a meaningful life. A meaningful life would include more positive experiences. More positive experiences will change the way your client thinks and feels.

But what about those activities your client is engaging in that are not helpful to him? Things like staying in bed much of the day, watching TV much of the day, eating too much, online gaming, to name just a few possibilities.

As your client is increasing meaningful, scheduled activities through an activity schedule, he should be decreasing depression-maintaining activities. The following activity is designed to help with this.

Target skill: Replacing depression-maintaining behaviors with meaningful behaviors. Insight about the role of meaningful behaviors in recovery.

1. Check in with your client. Ask him how the last week went. How is he feeling? Start with empathy. Listen compassionately. Use scaling questions like this one to track the intensity of his depression: On a scale from 1 to 10, with 10 being the highest, how would you rate your depression today? You may have to illustrate by explaining that a rating of 10 would mean your client is having constant thoughts of suicide and a rating of 1 would mean that your client is generally happy with very fleeting and few depressive thoughts and feelings.

2. Collaborate with your client on the next task: decreasing depression-maintaining activities. Find out what activities really trap your client in depression using Socratic questions. Here are some examples of Socratic questions related to this:

   - How do you feel after sleeping much of the day?

   - How does sleeping help you? How does it move you off track?

   - How do you feel after watching TV for much of the day?

   - How does watching TV help you? How does it move you off track?

   - How do you feel after playing Candy Crush (insert game of choice) for much of the day?

   - How does playing Candy Crush help you? How does it move you off track?

3. Review last week's homework: What scheduled activities did your client engage in? How hard was it to engage in those activities? What worked? What did not work? Continue to expand the intervention over time by scheduling more of what worked and increasing the frequency of doing what worked. Your client may want to try to meet with an old friend *and* look for a support group to join. Once your client is more engaged in meaningful activities, start moving into activities that will make a bigger difference:

Inspire your client to think about volunteering for a cause, or applying for a job. Again, there are many activity steps to take. Break things down into manageable steps.

4. Work on today's task: Go back to helping your client visualize what moves him forward and what maintains his depression.

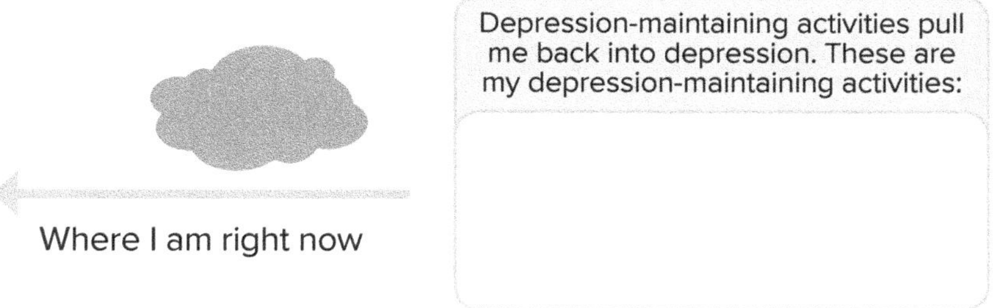

Figure 27

Create a list of depression-maintaining activities. Help your client pick one of those activities and create a schedule that decreases it. Once again: Think small steps. There is a reason why people engage in depression-maintaining activities. They feel safe. They require little effort. Lack of motivation in depression is not a personal fault, but rather a symptom of depression.

5. Create new activity schedule. If your client tends to play video games from 10 a.m. until 4 p.m. every day, change the schedule. Remember, if you take something away, you have to add something to fill the void. This is where increasing meaningful activities and decreasing depression-maintaining activities combine. Be sure to collaborate with your client on the replacement activity. It must be an activity that is less depression-maintaining, but that your client is willing to engage in.

Help your client think this way:

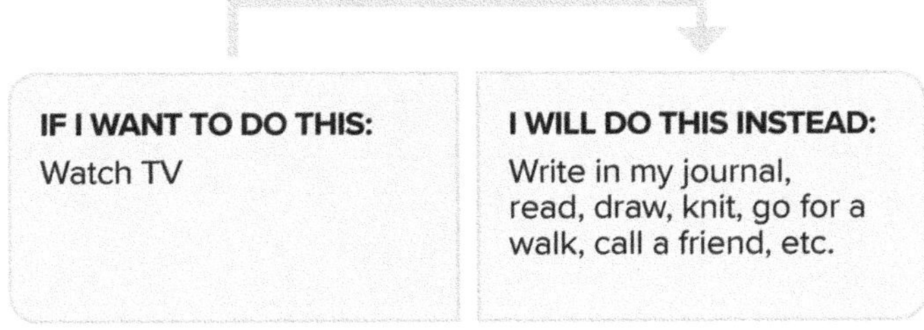

Figure 28

You may want to create an index card for your client to take home as a reminder. Be sure to identify more than one replacement activity, so your client can switch if he gets annoyed by or tired of one replacement activity.

6. Create a new activity schedule chart together with your client:

	Afternoon
Mon	Watch TV Instead: Create collage
Tue	Watch TV Instead: Go for a walk
Wed	Etc.
Thu	
Fri	
Sat	
Sun	

Figure 29

An empty version of this chart can be found in the appendix.

7. What if an activity schedule for several days is too much for your client? Once again, simplify. Use this chart:

Today's Activities
Time:
I usually do this:
Instead I will do this:

Figure 31

In order to successfully track activities with your client, you may want to staple a set of seven of these charts together.

8. Be sure to identify obstacles to taking away depression-maintaining activities with your client. Anticipate obstacles and develop ways of overcoming them. Perhaps your client needs an activity buddy? Help your client identify an activity buddy, someone who can help him stay on track. Be specific. Identify this person by name and make sure your client has a working phone

number for the activity coach. If your client can't identify anyone yet, help your client create coaching cards like this:

Today I will move in the direction of a meaningful life.

I can do this.

One step at a time.

Today I make my life better by ________________________________

____

____

____

Figure 32

While you are mainly trying to change what the client does, you are also working in the cognitive part of the cognitive triad when using coaching cards. You are trying to change your client's thinking about what he can do.

9. Be sure to set a goal for activity changing that your client can reach. If your client is watching TV every day all day it is not realistic to ask him not to watch TV at all. You may want to start by replacing 1 hour every day with a meaningful activity. You can then extend the time week by week.

10. Is it realistic to ask your client to never watch TV? There is nothing inherently wrong with watching TV or playing video games—in moderation. If things like watching TV or playing video games replace having a regular life, they become depression-maintaining activities. The goal is to move your client into a meaningful life.

11. Summarize what you have done today: You have identified depression-maintaining activities in your client's life and you have created a schedule to begin replacing these depression maintaining activities. You have done so by naming replacement activities. You have created a schedule to replace specific depression-maintaining activities with more meaningful activities.

12. Identify the homework with your client. Collaborate on a realistic goal and give your client the appropriate chart to complete. Once you have created the new activity schedule, this will serve as a monitoring chart. You are asking your client to do two things:

   - Engage in the agreed-upon replacement activity.

- Monitor how many times he has been successful with this. A simple check mark will do.
- Make a note when things did not work out. Why did they not work out? What got in the way?

13. Closing. Send your client home with words of encouragement like these:

   - *Getting rid of depression maintaining activities can be like sending home an unwanted houseguest. It's a relief.*
   - *Just keep moving toward the life you want. It can be built.*

INTERVENTION 5

Step into Life

This intervention is for depressed clients who are very physically inactive. It is about acknowledging and working with the body-mind connection. Not being physically active can be depression maintaining. The goal of this intervention is to help your client become appropriately physically active.

Be sure to check with your client about physical limitations. If your client has physical limitations, be sure to obtain a release of information from her primary care physician to ensure that your client is permitted to be physically active (the activity in this intervention is walking, not running). Once your client's physician has indicated that she is permitted to by physically active, be sure to make a case management note about this in her chart.

Target skill: Planning. Insight about the role of physical activity in decreasing depressive symptoms.

1. Start with empathy. Check in with your client about her level of depression. Use brief scaling questions to gauge her level of depression.

2. Collaborate with your client about today's task: becoming more active. Educate your client about the connection between a lack of physical activity and depression. Explain that inactivity can be a symptom of depression and can maintain depression.

3. Homework review: Explore with your client what went well with the homework and what did not. Was she able to replace depression-maintaining activities with more meaningful activities? How often? Is it time to step it up? Were there obstacles? And how did your client deal with the obstacles?

4. Work on today's task: Collaborate with your client on identifying ways in which she can become physically active. If she has been inactive for some time, this may be uncomfortable—it may even feel dangerous. Start by making a list like this:

Activity	Able to Do?
Get out of chair	
Stretch while standing	
Walk around apartment/space	
Walk down flight of stairs	
Walk around the block	
Walk a mile	
. . .	

Figure 33

Find out from your client what she is currently able to do. Then suggest that she try the "one step up" activity (the next activity down on the list). You may have to coach your client about this and even practice the activity in session.

This could mean that you coach your client through the discomfort of walking in the therapy space for a few minutes. It could also mean walking around the block with your client (ensure that she is OK with being seen with you). Or you could be showing your client a few simple stretches.

5. Lean into discomfort: Help your client identify obstacles.

    - If your client thinks she will look silly stretching, suggest that you stretch together. Tell her that you do not mind looking "silly" with her.

    - If your client expresses fear about increasing her activity level, make the next step even smaller. If your client feels that she cannot walk around her apartment with you, perhaps she can walk around her chair.

    - Help your client manage anxiety about her body. To your client it may feel like a slightly elevated heart rate is dangerous. Explain that the body is designed to cope with this and encourage her to give the activity a try anyway. If she does and completes the activity, give her lots of positive feedback about trying things that are uncomfortable.

6. Assign homework. Create a physical activity "prescription" based on what your client can do and has agreed to do. You could have a "prescription" pad like this:

Physical Activity "Prescription"							
Name:							
Date:							
Prescribed Activity:							
Dosage/Frequency:							
Time:							
Activity Completed:							

Figure 34

7. A checklist can be used to review success of the assignment. You are assigning physical activity (level tailored to your client) as homework.

8. Summarize for your client what you are trying to accomplish by adding physical activity to her daily schedule. If she has any questions, answer them now. If your client is hesitant, address this now or she will likely not complete the activity. It is better to take smaller steps than no steps at all.

9. Closing. Send your client home with supportive statements like these:

    - *You did great today. You even _______.*

    - *Practice makes perfect. Just take one step at a time.*

INTERVENTION 6

Making Music/Making sound

There is something very physical about making music. Music can be a great way to express feelings. Making music can be empowering. When you make music, you have a voice—your own or through an instrument. Finding one's voice can be a great way to become active when suffering from depression. This intervention requires that you, the therapist, become comfortable with making music. It does not require that you know how to sing or play an instrument.

Target skill: Communication. Comfort with oneself. Acceptance.

What you will need: You will need to be comfortable with singing or humming. Access to music by smartphone. Simple musical instruments like a small drum, keyboard, recorder, bells, etc.

1. Begin with empathy. Check in with your client. How is he feeling today? Use scaling questions to assess his current level of depression. Briefly touch on any changes in your client's life.

2. Identify today's task: having a voice and being heard. Explain that feeling down often results in being quiet and withdrawn, and sometimes angry. Explain that being too quiet or too angry is not a personal fault, but rather a symptom of depression that can be changed. Invite him to participate in an experiment in finding his voice through music.

3. Review last week's homework: What worked? How often did your client engage in the prescribed physical activity? Can he step it up and increase the frequency or move on to a more challenging activity?

4. Work on today's task: Explore with your client his comfort level with his voice. Is he comfortable with singing or humming a song with you? Perhaps it would be easier to sing along to a song you play on your phone? Or is it most comfortable to sing together?

   If singing is not an option, how about playing an instrument? You can easily create a set of drums out of plastic buckets and wooden sticks. Perhaps you can keep a keyboard in your office.

5. Find an instrument or voice activity that is comfortable for your client. Help your client engage in this activity. It is often easier to do this together. If your client lets you, join in with him, but be sure never to overpower his voice or his instrument.

6. Here are some suggestions about how to start:

   - Drumming: Ask your client to start with a simple beat. Then join him. Suggest that he establish a rhythm, and follow his lead. See what happens. Let things speed up or calm down.

   - Humming: You can start by humming a well-known children's song like "Row Your Boat" or "Wheels on the Bus." Ask your client to become louder with you. Make eye contact. See what happens.

- Singing: Ask your client to pick a song he would like to sing. Play it on your phone and karaoke it together. Can you get louder together? What happens when you look at each other?

7. Review the activity with your client. How did he feel? Was this fun? What was it like to become louder? What was it like to hear his own voice?

8. Explore with your client the possibility of finding her voice and becoming more active by speaking up for herself.

9. Explore with your client the possibility of using his voice or an instrument to simply feel alive and experience joy.

10. Summarize what you have done: You have explored ways in which your client can find his voice using his own voice or that of an instrument. You have engaged in this together and perhaps you got to know each other better in the process. You heard your client's voice and your client heard yours.

11. Assign homework: Ask your client to pick one musical activity to engage in on a daily basis. If your client has family members, ask him if he could include a family member (another step toward overcoming isolation).

Here is your prescription pad for musical activities:

Musical Activity "Prescription"						
Name:						
Date:						
Prescribed Activity:						
Dosage/Frequency:						
Time:						
Activity Completed:						

Figure 35

Once again, there is room on the pad for monitoring through checkboxes and this homework can be reviewed and expanded.

12. Be sure to check in with your client to answer any remaining questions. Encourage him to have fun with the activity and be adventurous. Send your client home with encouraging thoughts like these:

- *Having a voice can be fun.*
- *It's OK to laugh while learning to have a voice.*

Making Art/Making Meaning

Being creative is another way of being active. Music may not be right for everyone. Perhaps your client is more willing and able to create a visual representation of her reality. Keep in mind that the appearance of the project is less important than the process of creating it. The object of this intervention is for your client to become active, not to create a perfect work of art.

Be sure to have a variety of art materials available: Lots of paper, crayons, markers, and pencils. Old magazines for collages. Glue. Scissors. Modeling clay. You can also use natural materials such as branches, sticks and leaves to make art. You can incorporate stamps into an art project. Almost anything that is safe to use can be used to make art.

If your client wants a simple start, perhaps you can print out mandalas and have her color them.

Making art can be empowering as long as you can help your client let go of perfectionism.

Target Skills: Communication. Self-expression. Increasing meaningful activities.

What you will need: Art materials that suit your client. Nearby park or garden (optional).

1. Begin with empathy. Check in with your client. How is she feeling today? Use scaling questions to assess her current level of depression. Briefly touch on any changes in your client's life.

2. Identify today's task: becoming active through making art. Educate your client about what this means. Art is a form of expression. Art is communication. Art is play. Art is not about perfection.

3. Review last week's homework: Was your client able to engage in a musical activity at the scheduled time and frequency? If yes, does she want to step it up? Do more of what works, perhaps join a choir? If no, does she want to modify the activity or try another activity? Find out how your client felt during the activity. How did she feel at the beginning of the week about engaging in the activity? How about the end?

4. Work on today's task: Show your client all of the materials you have (or collect more natural materials outside—this would add the activity of walking). Ask her to pick materials she is comfortable with.

5. Because it can be uncomfortable to work alone, you should pick an art activity, too, but not the same one as your client. Be sure not to create a magnificent work of art. This would be intimidating for your client. You may want to color or create a doodle project.

   If your client needs help selecting materials, help her. If she needs ideas for a project or image, ask her what kinds of things she likes (perhaps her cat, kids, cars).

Another option is to tell your client to simply express how she feels using color or making a collage.

6. When your client has completed her project, compliment her for doing the work. Value her project. Ask her questions about it. Be sure that the project leads to a conversation and feelings of appreciation. Attune with your client's discomfort about making art (if there is any) and help her manage it. This is why it is so important that your own project be far less than perfect. Here are some things you can say:

    - *That looks amazing.*

    - *I am so impressed that you ___________.*

    - *I am so glad we can create art together.*

7. Summarize what you have done together: You have become active by creating an art project. Your client has created something unique. Art is one way to become active and make meaning in life. You have explored your client's comfort and discomfort about making art. You have helped your client understand and accept that her work has value. When you are done, ask your client what she will do with her project.

    - Will she hang it up at home?

    - Will she put it in a special box?

    - Will she carry it with her as a reminder of her ability to create something new?

8. Homework: Help your client identify a daily art activity. What would work for her at home? If making art at home feels intimidating, start with assigning coloring as homework. Once that feels comfortable, she can move on to a more complex activity. Be sure to always value any artwork your client brings into session to show you. If she cannot bring it in, ask her to take a picture with her phone. Use every opportunity to value your client's artwork. Depression makes you feel that nothing you do matters. Help your client understand and feel that her work matters.

Art Activity "Prescription"							
Name:							
Date:							
Prescribed Activity:							
Dosage/Frequency:							
Time:							
Activity Completed:							

Figure 36

Use the prescription pad for art activity monitoring.

9. Closing. Help your client value her own work by asking her to say one true and good thing about it, then respond by rephrasing what your client says about her work, but amplifying the positive even more.

Just Dance

Because depression can feel so heavy, it can be difficult for people with depression to keep moving. It may literally feel like movement is impossible, because every part of the body is weighed down by depression. For someone suffering from this heaviness of depression, it might seem impossible to experience joyful motion. The key to this intervention is to start small and to pick the right kind of music, something your client likes.

Target skill: Increasing meaningful activity. Joyful presence.

What you will need: Access to music (smartphone).

1. Begin with empathy. Check in with your client about her mood. Use simple scaling questions to help her gauge her current level of depression. It is important to embody hope for your client.

2. Identify today's task together with your client: Experiencing joyful movement. Explain the importance of paying attention to the body and becoming active. Explain that dancing is one way to become active. If your client hates dancing, simply change the words you use. Talk about motion or body movement.

3. Review last week's homework: Was your client able to engage in the art activity at the prescribed frequency? Is she ready to take the next step? Would she want to join an arts or crafts group? Volunteer to help children with art activities? Or were there barriers and she would rather be active in other ways? Be sure to be specific about what is next for your client and incorporate this into her activity schedule.

4. Work on today's task: Begin by asking your client about the kind of music she likes. Ask her to identify a specific song or piece of music or type of music. If your client is able to identify a specific song, play it for her on your phone. Listen together. If your client is a teenager or child, make sure that the song is age appropriate. If your client picks a song that reinforces depressive thoughts and feelings, help her reflect on this. You can explain that while the song may include validation of her feelings of depression, the kind of song you are looking for together is a song that will encourage joyful motion. Ask her for more song suggestions until you find a song that will work.

5. Ask her what she likes about the song: Is it the words? The music? Is it the beat? Play the song again after you have found out why your client likes it so much. Pay attention to the way she moves her body. Is she tapping her foot? Her fingers? Is any part of her moving to the music?

6. While the song is playing, continue to talk with your client about the song. Listen carefully for any meaning she derives from it and talk with her about creating meaning and purpose in life with the help of music.

7. Now, ask your client to dance or move to the music in any way that is comfortable and appropriate. For children and teens, you may have to set some clear limits here.

   Of course, you can't just watch. This would make your client more self-conscious. If your client is willing to tap her foot, do something similar.

8. Use eye contact to connect with your client. Is she embarrassed? Are you both laughing when you look at her? Just normalize the experience of moving to the music.

9. Explain that humans have used dance to express emotions and relieve stress through the ages. You and she are in good company when dancing.

10. If your client asks you how any of this relates to her depression, explain:

    - Depression lies to you.

    - Depression tells you that you can't and should not move.

    - Depression keeps you from experiencing joy through motion.

    - The only way to reconnect with joy through motion is to move.

    - Dance is one particular way of moving.

    - No one is watching.

    - It will take time to become comfortable.

   Ask her to start with what feels comfortable. If this means tapping her foot to the music, this is OK.

11. Summarize what you have done together: You have become active through moving to the music in spite of the heaviness of depression. Help her reflect on the experience of joy or discomfort this has brought her. If she expresses any connection with the meaning of a song, explain that making meaning is an important part of recovering from depression. Highlight moments of connection during the activity.

12. Assign homework: Use the prescription pad to help your client schedule dance/motion activities. Explain that it might be easiest if she sticks with the one piece of music/song for the next week to gain some comfort when moving. It will be easier if the music is predictable. Collaborate with your client on the frequency of the activity and the time, but generally speaking, scheduling the activity once a day is probably a good idea. Remind your client to check the "Activity Completed" box right after she has completed the activity, as this will serve as the basis for homework review the next time you meet.

Dance Activity "Prescription"							
Name:							
Date:							
Prescribed Activity:							
Dosage/Frequency:							
Time:							
Activity Completed:							

Figure 37

13. Closing. Encourage your client to:

- Have fun with the homework.
- Include family members or friends who would help her experience joy.
- Dance like no one is watching.

INTERVENTION 9

Doing for Others

Depression almost inevitably leads to isolation and inactivity. People with depression are often reluctant to do things for themselves. They may feel that they are undeserving of any meaningful activity. When asked about others, however, people with depression are often more able to admit that others may need and deserve help. Helping others can bring with it a sense of satisfaction. Helping others is a good way for someone with depression to become active.

Target skill: Increasing meaningful activity. Making meaningful connections.
What you will need: Community directory.

1. Check in with your client. How did the last week go? Use scaling questions to determine his current level of depression. Continue to embody hope. Pay attention to the small steps your client has taken during the last week to step out of depression. Be sure to talk with him about those small steps.

2. Collaborate with your client on identifying today's task: helping others. It is OK to be creative. It is, however, important that the activity of helping be a new one. Here is an example of what will not work:

    - Your client is a mother and is already overwhelmed by helping her children get ready for school and by their constant need for reassurance and emotional support. Clearly, helping the children more is not a great place to start. Here is what you could do instead: If your client likes animals, perhaps she can volunteer at the local animal shelter. An advantage of volunteering with animals is that they do not require conversation. They are just happy for you to hang out with them.

    - How about volunteering at the food pantry? Giving out food to those who need it (even if your client himself gets help there) can be very satisfying.

3. Review last week's homework: Ask your client to take out the dance activity "prescription pad." Take a look together. Did your client engage in the activity? Ask him what the experience was like. You can ask questions like these:

    - *When did you feel silly?*

    - *When did you feel joy?*

    - *How did you know you felt joy?*

    Listen for moments of joy and amplify those moments. Pay attention to your client's face. When you see the first hint of a smile, point this out, then ask him to continue to describe the experience. Ask how his body feels differently when he describes moments of joy.

4. Work on today's task: Identify the steps your client needs to take to engage in the activity of helping others. Be concrete, make a list. Help your client make phone calls. You may have to model the phone call for your client.

    Here is an outline of steps you could use with your client:

Getting ready to help__________________
Call ________
Find out what the organization needs
Determine if you are willing/able to do what is needed
Make an appointment to visit
Plan for getting there/back
Go to your first volunteer session

Figure 38

You can add anything else to the list.

5. Review with your client what you have done so far: You have identified a helping activity to engage in. You have made a step-by-step plan and taken the first few steps together. This is also a good time to explain again to your client how helping others can help him feel better. You may want to draw a vivid picture with words describing what the activity may look like. Here is an example of what this may sound like:

   - *Think for a moment about the dog you are walking. The dog does not get out much. The dog will be so excited.*

   - *Imagine holding the leash with the dog ready to go!*

   - *Now imagine coming back the second time. The dog will remember you and be even more excited. The dog knows you will take it outside.*

   - *You are doing a very good thing for this dog! You are helping the dog feel happy.*

6. Assign homework. This is where your "prescription pad" comes in handy again.

Helping Activity "Prescription"							
Name:							
Date:							
Prescribed Activity:							
Dosage/Frequency:							
Time:							
Activity Completed:							

Figure 39

Pick a dosage that will work for your client. Generally speaking, if the activity involves having to leave the house, something that may be difficult for your depressed client, set the dosage at once per week to begin with. Explain that it is a good idea to stick with a specific day and time weekly, as this will establish a rhythm (and most organizations prefer this for ease of planning). Once your client is comfortable with the activity, be sure to review it with him and step up the dosage (hours) or frequency (perhaps to twice a week).

If your client is currently not working, you can use any volunteer activity to explore his interest in future job-training planning.

7. Closing. Send your client home with encouraging words like these:

- *You can build meaningful connections by helping others.*

- *Helping others makes you feel good about yourself, because you are making a difference.*

- *If you can make a difference for others, you can make a difference for yourself, too.*

Doing for Oneself

Doing meaningful things for oneself can be difficult for someone suffering from depression. Depression is constantly conning your client into filling her time with things that temporarily numb the depression or keep it away from consciousness, such as sleeping, eating, watching TV, or playing video games. When your client is doing these things, she is not taking meaningful steps toward recovering.

Remember, there is nothing wrong with watching television or playing video games, but if these things are all your client does, it will be difficult to recover from depression. There is a life out there for your client to discover step by step.

Target skill: Recognizing needs. Increasing positive attention to self.

1. Begin with empathy. Check in with your client. Help her gauge her level of depression using simple scaling questions. Compliment her on her efforts to become more active.

2. Collaborate with your client on identifying today's task: doing something meaningful for herself. You may need to educate your client again about depression-maintaining activities.

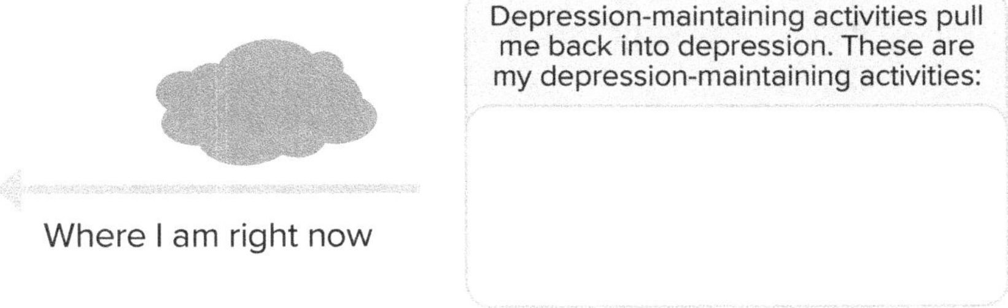

Figure 40

Help your client create a list of meaningful activities related to doing something for herself. Here are some examples:

- Take a bubble bath (to make the body feel better).
- Visit a beautiful place.
- Look at images of beautiful places.
- Go to a place you have never been before, such as a forest or lake.
- Sit outside and feel the sun on your skin.
- Meet up with a friend.

3. Homework review: Review with your client what went well during the last week. Define success as simply engaging in the helping activity. Explore what your client liked about the activity. Pay close attention to your client's nonverbal communication. What does she look like when she talks about

the activity? Do you see evidence of enjoyment? If you do, tell her about what you are seeing. You may want to say something like:

- *I just saw a twinkle in your eye when you were talking about that dog.*

- *You had a bit of a smile on your face when you were talking about reading to the little boy at the library.*

4. Work on today's task: Take a look at the list your client has created. Help her weed out the things that are either too difficult or not possible right now (such as taking an expensive trip). Narrow things down to the best activity that is actually possible.

5. Once you have identified that activity, begin working with your client on what is needed to complete the activity. If your client wants to take a bubble bath but can't afford to buy a fancy bottle of bubbles, improvise. Shampoo will do just as well! If your client wants to visit a beautiful place, pick a place that is within a reasonable range and help her plan how to get there. Be specific, as this will increase the likelihood of your client actually engaging in the activity.

6. Summarize with and for your client what you have done so far: Your client has picked a meaningful activity to engage in. You have created a list of things that are needed to engage in that activity. The purpose of the activity is to find enjoyment in real-life activities (as opposed to experiencing artificial joy through gaming or television).

7. Assign homework: It is time for your "prescription" pad again.

Meaningful Activity "Prescription"							
Name:							
Date:							
Prescribed Activity:							
Dosage/Frequency:							
Time:							
Activity Completed:							

Figure 41

Collaborate with your client on the frequency and time of the activity. For this activity, it is not necessary that your client engage in it often (though that would be great), but rather that your client engage in it mindfully and with the purpose of doing something good for herself.

8. What if your client is worried that she may feel guilty about doing things for herself? What if she feels she does not deserve it?

   You can explore the automatic thought "I don't deserve this" with your client, but do not spend too much time on this for now. Simply tell your client that depression can be a liar, and to acknowledge and then tune out automatic thoughts of being undeserving. Otherwise, you may spend a lot of time refuting the idea that your client is undeserving and very little time helping your client take a leap of faith into doing something meaningful for herself.

9. Closing. Send your client home with words of encouragement like these:

   - *You deserve to do good things for yourself.*

   - *You are learning to take good care of yourself.*

   - *This takes practice. But practice makes perfect.*

INTERVENTION 11

Speaking the Truth of Depression

When depression strikes, it often takes away a sense of home. Depression often isolates the person it afflicts. He may have no one to talk to, or may believe that no one would listen. This intervention targets the "unspeakableness" of depression. You, the provider, have to be willing to listen to things that are difficult to hear. One example of this is the desire to cease to be, the wish for it all to be over. Your gut may tell you to quickly talk with your client about why life is worth living, before listening to what he really has to say.

Listening to the voice of despair is not the same as endorsing despair. When your client talks about despair, be sure to listen with empathy and kindness. Thank him for sharing his thoughts and feelings with you.

The very act of sharing the thoughts and feelings of depression, the act of communication about depression, is a step out of depression, because your client now is no longer alone. There is one caveat: If your client is getting graphic about how he would commit suicide, if he talks about details of committing suicide, if he seems drawn to describing exactly what he would do, it is time to move into safety planning. After you have determined that your client is struggling with suicidal thoughts and plans, guide your client away from the graphic description of suicide, using these explanations:

- *Talking about this in such graphic detail is not healing. It reinforces the idea of suicide. It keeps you focused on the idea of self-harm. For your safety, we need to move away from this conversation into planning for your safety.*

- *The idea that you need to die is one of those lies that depression tells you. You don't need to die. You deserve to live. You have the right to live a meaningful life. This is something we can build together.*

Target skill: Communication. Honesty.

What you will need: Ability to listen reflectively without interrupting. Ability to take in and co-regulate intense emotions.

1. Begin with empathy. Check in with your client about the last week. Use simple scaling questions to assess his level of depression. Ask about experiences that stood out. Validate client feelings of depression, but also highlight moments of joy and connection.

2. Collaborate with your client about identifying today's task: speaking the truth of depression. Ask your client if he has ever felt rejected when talking about his depression. Does it seem like people do not want to listen to him anymore? They just want him to get better, but they do not want to acknowledge how difficult depression can be?

3. Review last week's homework: Was your client able to engage in the positive activity for himself at the agreed-upon frequency? How did he feel when he did? If he did enjoy the activity, you may want to step it up for the following week and add another activity from the list to his activity schedule. If he did

not engage in the activity at the agreed-upon frequency, what stood in the way? Redefine success: Success means that your client tried! If the activity was not right and not comfortable, pick a different one.

4. Work on today's task: Explain to your client that you will listen to his thoughts and feelings about depression—even those that others may not want to listen to. Explain that you are listening, because you don't want him to be and feel alone with those thoughts and feelings. When your client begins to talk about his depression, simply listen and validate. You are not validating that he is alone, you are validating that he is feeling alone. You can say simple things like:

   - *I hear you.*
   - *Tell me more.*
   - *Is there more?*
   - *That must be difficult.*

5. You may want to take notes of what your client is saying.

6. Listen and validate until your client is done. Do not offer solutions yet. When your client is done, ask one more time: *Is there anything else?*

7. Now, reflect back to your client what he has told you. Frequently ask: *Did I get this right?* Let him correct you and add things. When you are done, ask: *Did I forget anything*?

8. Once you are done reflecting your client's thoughts and feelings back to him, ask him what it felt like to hear you validate his thoughts and feelings by saying them out loud. Wonder out loud about the experience of sharing. You can say: *Now that you have shared the truth of your depression, you are no longer alone in it.*

9. Thank him for sharing his experience of depression with you. Explain that it is possible to communicate about depression even when depression itself tells you that it is not.

10. Summarize what you have done so far: Your client has told you about his feelings of depression. You have listened and validated his feelings. He has been able to communicate how depression feels and you now understand his depression better. This also means that your client is no longer completely isolated, because he has shared his experience.

11. Collaborate with your client on developing homework: Help him identify who he can try to share his experiences of depression with. Who is a good listener? Who is able to carry this without feeling distressed? If your client can't think of a family member or friend, think about connecting him with a support group such as NAMI, or explore his connection (if any) with a supportive faith community. Ask your client to share his experience of depression with one trustworthy person and be mindful of the experience.

12. If your client is not ready to talk with anyone outside of treatment about his depression, ask him to write his thoughts down in this manner:

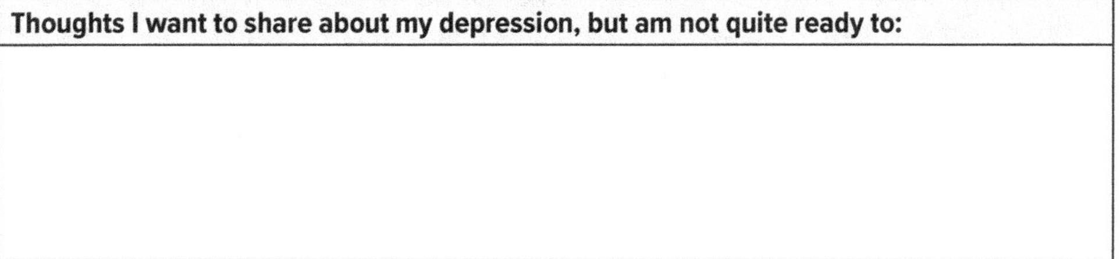

Figure 42

Ask your client to bring this list to your next meeting so that you can help his practice communicating about depression.

13. Closing: Thank your client for communicating about his depression. Reinforce the idea that communicating about depression decreases isolation. You can say:

- *We share an understanding of your depression now.*

- *Sharing with others makes us feel more connected.*

- *Connection helps decrease feelings of depression.*

- *This week, give sharing a try.*

Moving Forward

Depression has a way of maintaining itself. You don't have to do much to stay depressed. If your client does nothing, she will likely stay depressed. Doing nothing has great allure. It is always easier than doing something.

Moving from doing very little (watching television/playing video games) to doing something meaningful, therefore, is not an easy task.

If your client is employed, she might be so tired and burned out after work that it truly feels like she can't do anything. If your client is able to work, this is already a mammoth achievement. You should let her know that you understand how difficult it can be for her to just get up and get going in the morning. The following intervention is about envisioning change in order to create change.

Target skill: Meaning making. Planning. Becoming active.

1. Begin with empathy. Check in with your client about her level of depression using simple scaling questions. What went well last week?

2. Collaborate with your client on identifying today's task: envisioning change in spite of the pull of depression. You can use questions like these: *What if depression was suddenly gone? What would be different? What would you be doing?*

3. Homework review: Was your client able to share the truth of her depression with someone? What did this feel like? Or was she able to write some things down for the two of you to talk about? If she did, explore those things with her. Doing so will help her understand that it is possible to communicate about depression. Reinforce that communicating about depression can lift some of the loneliness.

4. Work on today's task: moving forward. Return to the key question: What would be different if your client was no longer depressed? What would she be doing? You can use this image to help your client think about moving forward:

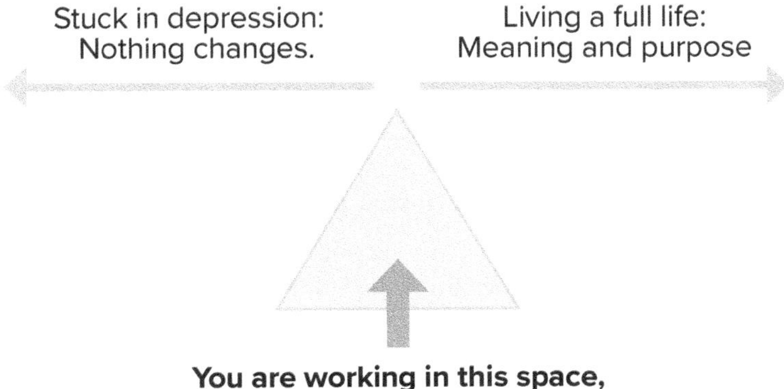

Figure 43

Moving forward means taking one step at a time in the direction of a full life. Steps don't have to be gigantic. By taking many small steps, you can get there. A full life does not happen, it is built. If it is built, then she can build it!

5. It is good to keep in mind the kind of life your client envisions by taking a look at the answers to the key questions. But how can your client get to a meaningful life—how can anyone? Work with your client on three concrete steps she can take in the direction of a meaningful life in the following week. You can use this image to record the three steps for your client:

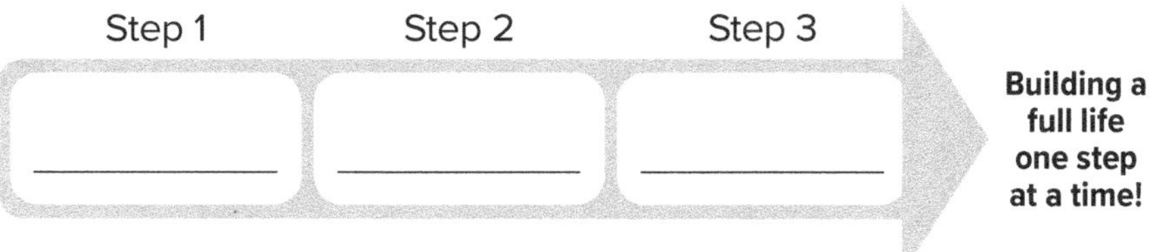

Figure 44

- What if your client struggles with identifying any steps?
- Go back to her answers to the key questions. Perhaps your client wants to be in a relationship, but she currently spends much of her time in her apartment.
- Here are some examples of steps she could take:
  - Join a class.
  - Join a support group.
  - Attend a family gathering.
  - Go to a PTA meeting

You get the idea: If your client stays in her apartment, there is very little chance she will meet someone. If she "gets out there," even in small ways, her chances increase.

What if your client is so depressed that she tells you she can't do anything?

Go back to the idea (you are now doing some cognitive work) that depression is a con man and a thief. In all likelihood it just feels like your client can't do anything. Explain that not everything she is thinking and feeling is true. You can use the following technique to demonstrate.

Ask your client to say "I can't wave at you" while waving her hand at you. Explain that just because we think, feel, or say something, it does not mean that this is true. The mind makes stuff up all the time!

6. Summarize what you have done together: By using the key questions you have determined what kind of a life your client wants. Your client now understands that a full life is built and that she can take small steps to build

one. You have identified the three small steps your client has agreed to take toward a full life.

7. Assign homework: Give your client an index card with the identified steps and ask her to check off the steps once she has completed them.

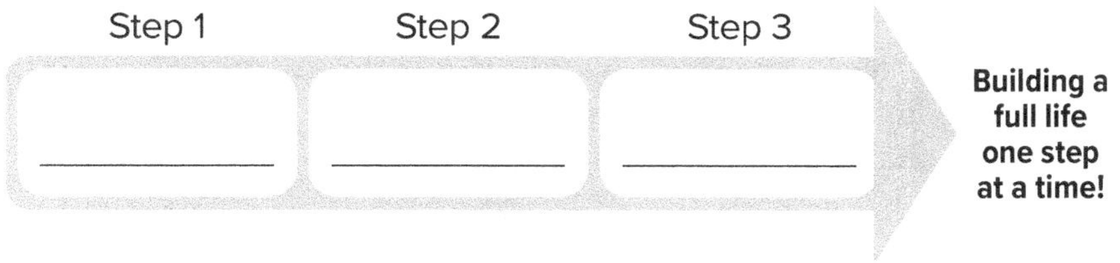

Figure 45

Check in with your client. Does she understand the homework? What went well today? Are there any barriers to completing the homework? If there are, be sure to identify steps your client can take to remove the barriers. Perhaps she agreed to take a step that now feels too large to take? Make it smaller and more manageable!

8. Closing. Send your client home with kind words. You can say:

    - *Even small steps get you closer to the life you want.*

    - *Lots of small steps turn into big changes.*

INTERVENTION 13

Being Kind

Depression does not make one kinder. When people are depressed they often judge themselves and others in harsh ways. Depression can bring anger to the surface much quicker. This intervention starts with the practice of being kinder to others. Many of our clients find it difficult to be kind to themselves. Being kinder to others can bring kindness into your client's life in return.

Target skill: Compassion and connection. Stepping out of isolation. Building relationships.

1. Begin with empathy. Check in with your client about the past week. What went well? What did not?

2. Collaborate with your client on identifying today's task: being kind to others, even if I perceive them not to be kind to me. The task is to simply put out some good into the world, to make a positive contribution in a world that can be harsh. If your client has any objections to this, he can voice them now. If his objections are based in depressive thinking (once again, you are doing some quick cognitive work), remind him that depression is a con man. If depression is telling him that everyone is awful, this is most certainly not true, objectively speaking. Most babies are not awful!

3. Check in about the homework: Take a look at your client's checklist together. Was he able to take three steps towards a full life? If he was, be sure to have him tell you about his successes, no matter how small.

4. What if he completed his three steps, but feels no different? Explain to your client that taking pleasure in things will follow with time. For now it is important that he has taken the steps. Praise him. If he was not able to derive pleasure from taking the steps, perhaps he can from being praised by you!

5. What if your client did not complete his three steps, or completed only one of them? Stay positive. Celebrate what your client has done. Identify barriers and make a new plan. Embody hope.

6. Work on today's task together: What does it mean to be kind? What does kindness look like in action? Ask your client to give you some examples of how others have been kind to him.

7. What if your client says no one has ever been kind to him? Ask him to think about a situation in which someone was not kind to him. Ask him to tell you what kindness would have looked like in that situation. Ask him to be specific: What should the person have done and said? When he answers the question, compliment him for his understanding of kindness. Say: *If you know kindness, then you know how to be kind.*

8. Make a plan with your client for being kind to someone. Be specific. Ask your client to pick a person he will be kind to. Map out the situation. What will he say to that person? What will he do?

Here is a chart you can use to help your client map out kindness:

Mapping Out Kindness
Completed ?
Where?
When?
What will I say?
What will I do?

Figure 46

What if your client is worried about that person's response?

- If your client is choosing to be kind to someone who is likely going to be mean in return, choose a different person!

- Explain to your client that this exercise is not about the other person, but about him and the good he can do in the world. If the person returns his kindness by being mean, he can just walk away. It's a good life skill to learn.

9. Summarize with and for your client what you have done so far: You have identified what it means to be kind and made a plan for your client to be kind to a specific person.

10. You can now assign homework by handing your client the completed Mapping Out Kindness chart. Ask your client to check the checkbox once he has completed the act of kindness and bring the chart to your next meeting.

11. Closing. Check in with your client. What went well today? Does he have any questions? Foresee any barriers to completing the task? Be sure to help your client identify ways to overcome barriers before he leaves, or he is unlikely to complete the homework.

INTERVENTION 14

Starting Right Here

This intervention is for those clients who struggle with maintaining order in their homes because of their depression. You may see piles of unwashed clothing or dishes or unopened mail. Perhaps the trash has not been taken out for quite some time. There is an odor coming from the cat box, and your client herself may look unkempt. This intervention is to help your client begin somewhere with creating a sense of control over her life. Once again, depression has lied to her and convinced her that it is all too much and can't be done. Your job is to help your client start "right here."

Target skill: Planning. Becoming active one step at a time. Insight about depression-maintaining activities and environments.

1. Begin with empathy. Check in with your client about her level of depression using simple scaling questions. How has your client been since your last meeting?

2. Collaborate with your client on identifying today's task: starting right here. Explain that "starting right here" means taking action, however small, to gain control over one aspect of one's life, to accomplish one thing. If your client tells you that it is all pointless and can't be done, remind her that depression can convince her of things that are not true. You may want to ask her to move her chair an inch to the left. If she can accomplish that, who is depression to tell her that she can't accomplish anything?

3. Review the homework with your client: Was she able to be kind to the person chosen? If she was, what happened when she was kind? Was it difficult? Was the person surprised? Did the person say anything? How did it feel to be kind, independent of how the person reacted? If your client was not able to be kind, what stopped her? Can you change the task, perhaps pick a different person? Perhaps your client can choose someone she does not know, such as a store clerk.

4. Begin working with your client on today's task. Where could she start actively creating a sense of agency and order in her life? Look around together!

   Here are some ideas for possible starting points:

   - Taking care of self: Wash and comb hair, put on fresh clothes.

   - One less pile: Wash and fold a pile of clothes, then put it away.

   - One clean surface: Empty and clean the kitchen counter or the bathroom counter.

   - Bag and ditch it: Empty the cat box or trash and take to the dumpster.

   How does any of this affect the client's level of depression? Piles, dirt, and disorder have a way of growing. After a while it may seem that there is just no point in starting to clean up. But this is just another one of the lies depression tells. It can, in fact, be done—one step at a time.

5. Here is how chaos can feed into depression:

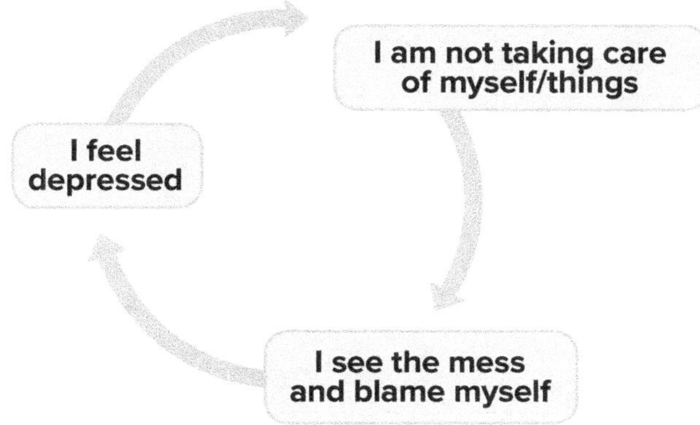

Figure 47

6. The goal is to get your client to start somewhere to interrupt this cycle. Help her identify where she can and would like to start. Explain that you would like to help her change the cycle to this:

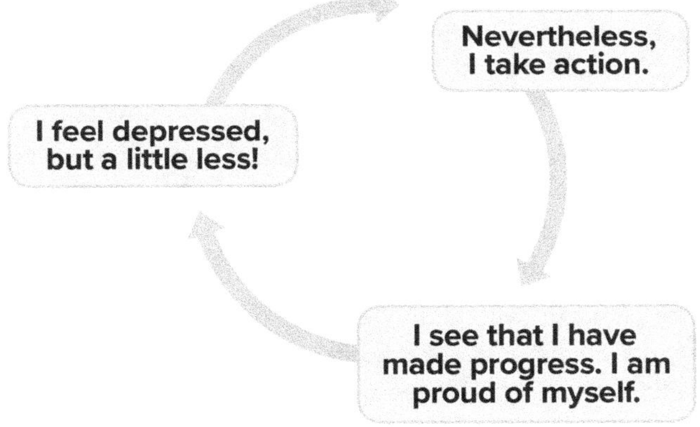

Figure 48

Help your client pick the one thing she can do. Be sure that this is something she can actually do. It is very unlikely that she will be able to clean the entire apartment in one day. But every day she can do one thing. Here is a template you can use to help her create a list. If your client struggles with writing, you can write for her or she can draw.

The one thing I am going to do:
Monday:
Tuesday:
Wednesday:
Thursday:
Friday:

Figure 49

It is a good idea to connect the tasks from one day to another. If your client cleans the bathroom sink counter on Monday, perhaps she can clean the toilet on Tuesday, take the bathroom trash out on Wednesday, and so forth. Within 5 days, she will have created a reasonably clean bathroom.

7. Summarize with and for your client what you have done so far: You have made a plan for your client to be an active agent in her life, beginning "right here." She has identified a task for every day and made a plan to complete it.

8. Assign homework: Give your client the template with the identified tasks. Ask her to check the task off with a check mark when it is completed. Explain that the point of the task is not to create perfection, but rather to get started and to regain the sense that things can get done—this is what depression has taken from her.

9. Closing. Check in again with your client. Are there any barriers to her completing the tasks she has picked? If there are, be sure to help her identify ways of removing the barriers or help her pick a new task. The key is to plan for success!

INTERVENTION 15

Starting with Me: Being Kind to Myself

Depression has a way of undermining the self. Depression sends perpetual messages to your client telling him how unworthy he is (core belief) and that it is all his fault (automatic thought). This intervention targets the behavioral component of the core belief of unworthiness.

The focus of this intervention is less on your client's automatic thoughts (though they matter) and more on how he can actually be kind to himself through active acts of kindness. Being compassionate toward oneself is quite different from self-pity. Self-pity simply maintains depression. Self-compassion results in acts of kindness toward oneself.

Target skill: Active self-compassion.

1. Begin with empathy. Check in with your client about his current level of depression using simple scaling questions. Has anything changed since the last meeting?

2. Collaborate with your client on identifying today's task: being kind to himself. Explain that you are looking less for positive self-affirmations (though these are great to combat negative automatic thoughts) and more for acts of kindness toward himself. Find out how your client feels about this, but do not dwell on his feelings extensively.

3. Review the homework: Take a look at the "one thing I am going to do" template and review with your client what he has done. Was he able to complete some of the tasks? Perhaps all of them? Celebrate with your client what he has done. Inquire about barriers to those tasks he did not complete. What got in the way? Should the task be replaced? Or can the barrier be overcome?

4. Work with your client on today's task: How can he be kind to himself? Begin by identifying with your client specific acts of self-kindness he can engage in. Here are some examples:

   - Write a kind note to yourself, place it on your nightstand, and read it in the morning.

   - Pick some wildflowers and put them on the kitchen table.

   - If it is sunny, go outside, stretch toward the sun, and let the sun "hug" you.

   - Ask your best friend to write a kind note for you. Tape it to your bathroom mirror and read it every time you look in the mirror.

   - Schedule mindful moments three times per day. During the mindful moment, look at the flowers on your kitchen table (or something similar) and just breathe.

   - Gently massage your temples.

   - Soak your feet in warm bubble water.

5.   Create a "being kind to myself" chart with your client. You can use this template to fill in:

Being kind to myself:	Done
Monday:	
Tuesday:	
Wednesday:	
Thursday:	
Friday:	

Figure 50

Have some fun while creating the list. When identifying a way for the client to be kind to himself, evoke the feeling of the activity with and for your client. Ask what it would be like to receive a kind note every day. Be sure to only include kind activities your client will actually enjoy. Those are the ones that make him smile while you are both talking about them.

You have two choices: You can vary the activity every day if your client likes variety, or you can repeat the same activity every day if your client likes simplicity.

6.   Summarize with and for your client what you have done so far: You have created a list of acts of self-kindness that your client can engage in. You have completed the acts of kindness chart. You have talked about what it would be like for your client to be kind to himself. Reassure your client that he is deserving of kindness, from himself and others. If he feels awkward about being kind to himself, ask him to take a leap of faith and simply try. This intervention is about taking action.

7.   Identify the homework: Give your client the "being kind to myself" chart and ask him to complete it over the next week. Ask him to check off each daily task once he has completed it.

8.   Closing. Be sure to check in with your client before he goes home about any obstacles that stand in the way. Did your client choose an activity he can't complete because he can't afford it? Change that activity before he leaves. The key for this activity is to plan for success. Leave your client with words of encouragement. You can say:

   - *You deserve kindness.*

   - *Being kind to yourself takes practice.*

   - *Just give it a try and see what happens when you are kind to yourself.*

Interventions Targeting the Cognitive Component of the Cognitive Triad

Interventions outlined in this chapter are aimed at creating change through examining the way your client thinks. This includes examining the more readily accessible automatic thoughts as well as your client's core beliefs. Keep in mind that while you are working with your client on targeting his cognitions, you are also targeting his emotions and his behaviors. Think of thoughts, feelings, and behaviors as the three strands of a braid. You can separate the three strands out, but in real life they are often interwoven.

The goal of all of these kinds of interventions is to ensure that your client's thoughts "fit" the situation. If there is a mismatch of the situation and your client's thoughts, you want your client to realize this, then adjust her thinking. Many of our clients are attached to the idea (again, just a thought) that just because they think something, this thought is true. The strand that binds many of the interventions together is this:

A thought is just a thought. A thought can be right, meaning it matches the situation it is attached to. A thought can also be wrong, meaning that is does not match the situation it is attached to. A thought can be a fabrication. A depressive thought can be a lie, a brain burp, or the brain's junk mail.

INTERVENTION 16

Stream of Thoughts

Target skill: Insight about the nature and role of thoughts. Ability to monitor thoughts.

1. Start with empathy. Check in with your client about her level of depression using simple scaling questions. Ask her about her thoughts about the last week. Ask her about what she did. These two questions will lay the foundation for differentiating between thoughts and actions.

2. Collaborate with your client about identifying today's task: becoming aware of all kinds of thoughts floating through her consciousness. Explain that today you are thought collectors. You are conducting an experiment. Your client can choose a subject, and you and she will "collect" her thoughts.

3. Review last week's homework: Was your client able to be kind to herself by taking kind actions? If she was, how did it feel? Did it feel surprisingly comforting? Did kindness affect her mood? If she was not able to be kind to herself, explore with her why not. What were the barriers? If your client is able, explore why it was difficult to be kind to herself. Does your client need to experience more kindness from others before she can be kind to herself?

4. Work together on today's task: Be thought collectors. It is best to have your client pick one subject, then ask her to think about it and say out loud every thought she has. You will be the scribe. You will write down all of her thoughts for 2–3 minutes. Be prepared to be a fast writer. Humans have a lot of thoughts. Give your client permission to follow her thoughts as the subject changes. Your client may choose the subject of "getting a bad grade at school" and end up talking about forgetting to buy groceries for dinner. Ask your client not to censor herself. It is OK to have and comment on thoughts that do not seem to make sense.

5. Collect your client's thoughts on a piece of paper. When she has completed her stream of thoughts, take out a large piece of paper and map her thoughts. This could look something like the following diagram:

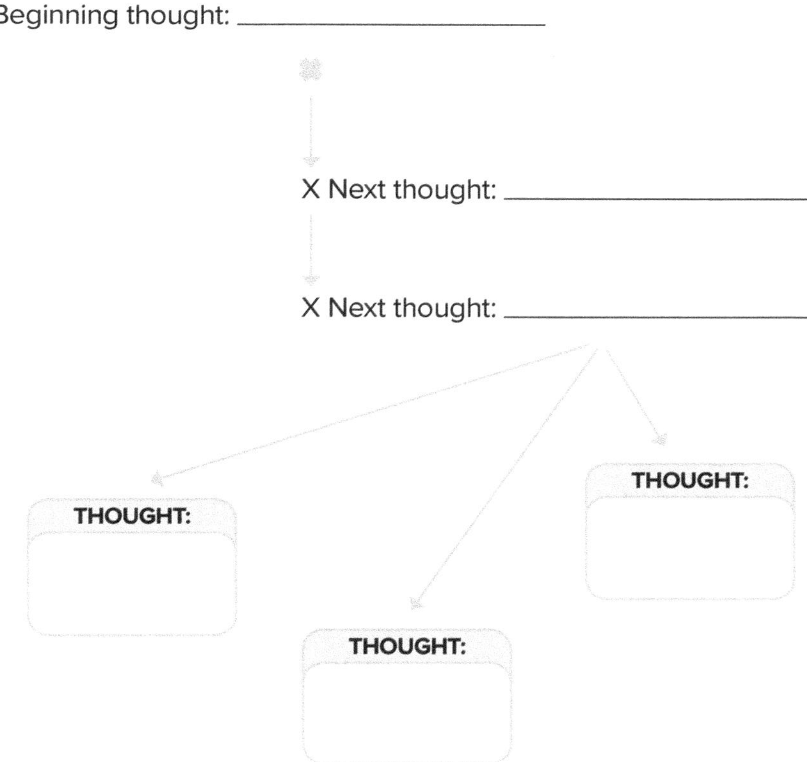

Figure 51

Keep branching out as needed.

Some thoughts may not connect to others in obvious ways or in any way. That is OK.

6. Once you have finished the thought map, take a look at it with your client. Are there any random thoughts? Any thoughts she finds weird? Or unwanted? Or wonderful? Any thoughts she wants to banish? Any funny thoughts?

7. Help your client reflect on her brain producing all of these thoughts. Say something like this:

> *Take a look at all of these thoughts we produce at humans. We are capable of producing relevant thoughts and random thoughts, funny thoughts and scary thoughts, logical thoughts and weird thoughts.*

8. Ask your client which of the many thoughts that went through her mind she is most focused on right now. Ask her if this means that it is the most important thought. In all likelihood it is not. It could be a thought about something very nice, or something frightening or embarrassing. Explain that our brains often home in on negative thoughts, even when they are random. There are feelings attached to the thought, so our focus goes to that one thought instead of another one.

9. Summarize with your client what you have done so far: You have collected your client's thoughts in an experiment. You have mapped her thoughts and you have determined that there are all kinds, including some that are random, illogical, and irrelevant. You have stepped back and taken a look at your client's thoughts from afar. You have observed the thought process. Ask your client what this was like!

10. If you are working with a child or someone who needs something more concrete, use the image of a tree and invite your client to decorate the branches with her thoughts.

Figure 52

Or she could draw apples on the tree to represent thoughts.

11. For the more technologically minded: Most phones have a recording function. Your client could simply record her thoughts on her phone and then create the thought map or tree from the recording. If your client is a child, a parent/caretaker will have to assist.

12. Assign homework: Give your client an empty thought map/tree drawing. Ask her to be a scientist for 2–3 minutes once this week and record her thoughts. When she is done, she should take a look at her thought map/tree and observe what thought her mind chooses to focus on. Ask her to circle that thought and bring her thought map/tree with her to your next meeting.

13. Closing. Summarize again what you have done today. Check in with your client to make sure that she understands the assignment and that there are no barriers to completing it. If your client feels that she cannot complete the assignment by herself, ask her if a friend or family member could assist with

recording her thoughts. Leave your client with words of encouragement. You can say:

- *Watching our thoughts can be interesting.*

- *It can help us track what we focus on.*

- *When we understand how our thoughts work, we can choose to focus on an important thought and let the other thoughts go.*

INTERVENTION 17

A Thought Is Just a Thought

This intervention builds on the prior one. Your client has learned that it is possible to step away from thoughts and observe them. He has learned that thoughts can be random and that we assign attention and or importance to some of them. The following intervention is designed to help your client recognize that a thought is just a construct of the mind that can be true and relevant to a situation, or not true and disconnected from a situation.

Target skill: Thought evaluation. Insight. Recognition of unhelpful automatic thoughts.

What you will need: Balloon to blow up. Sharp object to pop balloon.

1. Begin with empathy. Check in with your client about his current level of depression using simple scaling questions. Ask your client about any depressive thoughts he has had since your last meeting. Have any of them be persistent. If so, what are those persistent and pesky thoughts?

2. Collaborate with your client on identifying today's task: learning to step back another step by clearly labeling thoughts as thoughts, or more clearly, as "just" thoughts. Because we as humans identify ourselves as thinkers, we can be very attached to each thought we have. What if our thoughts were just thoughts? What if each thought went through a vetting process like this:

   - Is this thought relevant?

   - Does this thought match the situation?

   - Does this thought align with my values?

   - Is this a helpful thought?

3. Review last week's homework: Take a look at your client's thought map/tree. What kinds of thoughts do you see? Let your client tell you how he feels about each one. In this manner you are helping your client begin to understand the connection between thoughts and feelings (you are doing a little bit of work on the emotional component of the cognitive triangle). Reinforce for your client that he is able to observe his thoughts, that his thoughts are not identical with him.

4. Work with your client on today's task: List all the unwanted, unhelpful, unpleasant, untrue thoughts that have come to your client's mind. Many of them may be automatic thoughts, some may be core beliefs. If it is helpful, you may want to give your client the following definition of what an automatic thought is:

   - An automatic thought is a pesky, persistent, and often rapid-fire thought you did not ask for.

   - Automatic thoughts are often not helpful, because they do not match the situation you are in.

- Generally speaking, automatic thoughts tell you that you are unworthy, unlovable, and incompetent.

- Automatic thoughts, just like any thought, can be examined and dismissed.

You should end up with a list of three to five pesky thoughts.

5.   Ask your client to read each thought to you. After each, say to your client: *This is just a thought. It is not relevant to the situation. It is not true.*

6.   Once you have completed this part of the intervention, you will be the one to read the pesky thoughts to your client. It will be his job to say to you: "This is just a thought. It is not even relevant. It's like a brain hiccup. It is not true." It is OK to vary the words to fit your client.

7.   If there is a particularly nasty recurring thought, you can suggest that he can flush it down the toilet where it belongs. It's OK to do this together. You can say something like this: *There goes that pesky thought, down to the sewer where it belongs.*

8.   There are many other ways to symbolically get rid of or contain a pesky thought: Throw it in the garbage, lock it up, or rip it up.

9.   Explain to your client that perhaps the most powerful way to disarm a pesky thought is to realize that it is just a thought. It holds no power in itself if we don't give it power. In other words: A thought really is just a thought.

If you are working with a child, you could blow up a balloon. The balloon stands for a pesky thought. You can make it really big. You can get all worked up about the thought and blow up the balloon more and more. And then you can deflate it, by letting it go. So far you have held it shut with your fingers. When you let it go, it loses all the air. It deflates, it can't go anywhere. In the same way, you can deflate a pesky thought.

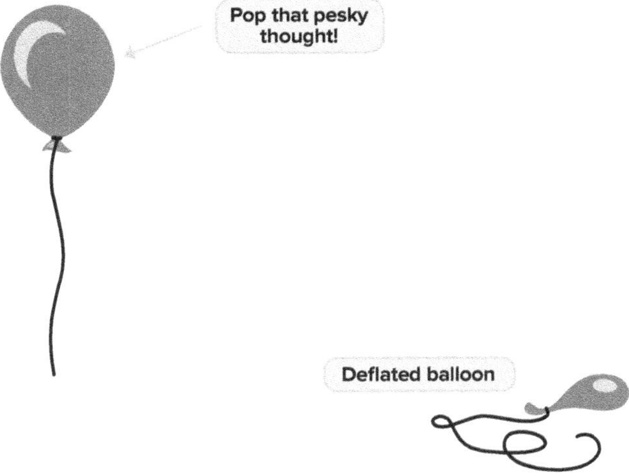

Figure 53

10. Summarize what you have done so far: You have learned that thoughts are just thoughts. You have learned that some thoughts can be pesky. They keep popping up even if they are irrelevant and not true. You have learned that those thoughts can be "put in place." They can also be deflated like a balloon.

11. Explain that this does not mean that your client has to run away from pesky thoughts. He is just not giving them the power to control how he feels and acts.

12. Assign homework: Ask your client about the most pesky, unpleasant thought in his life, the one that likely pops up every day. Give your client this handout as homework:

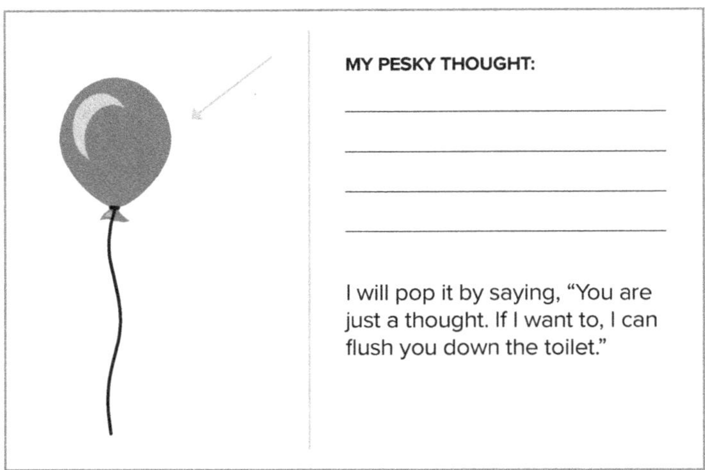

Figure 54

13. Closing. Check in with your client again. Make sure he understands the assignment. If he wants to, he can carry the homework handout in his pocket. In this way he can remind himself what to do about pesky thoughts as they arise. Ask your client if he has any questions about the assignment and wish him happy pesky-thought popping!

INTERVENTION 18

Show Me the Money!

This intervention dives further into examining the utility and truthfulness of a thought by looking at the evidence supporting and disproving it. Another way of thinking about this intervention is to ask: Is this a penny kind of a thought or a hundred-dollar-bill kind of thought? Where is this thought going to get me?

Target skill: Ability to evaluate thoughts. Defusion from unhelpful thoughts.

1. Begin with empathy. Check in with your client about her level of depression during the prior week. Ask her about pesky thoughts and depression. Can she see a connection?

2. Collaborate with your client on identifying today's task: Explain that you will be working together on identifying what a thought is worth by assigning it a monetary value. Ask her to think about what a penny thought might be and what a hundred-dollar thought might be.

3. Review last week's homework: Was your client able to pop or deflate her very pesky thought? If she was, how did it feel? Inquire about how real it felt to get rid of a thought in this manner. Did the thought come back? If it did, what did she do? If the thought came back, does this mean she did not do well? Explain that pesky automatic thoughts will continue to come, and she can continue to pop or deflate them. This does not mean that she is failing. The brain will continue to produce pesky thoughts. But she can keep evaluating thoughts, calling their bluffs and sending them away.

4. Work on today's task: Explain to your client that you are going to take a deeper look at some of her pesky thoughts with her and examine them for their worth.

    Here is how you are going to determine how much a thought is worth:

    -   If the thought fits the situation and is realistic and helpful, then the thought is worth $100.

    -   If the thought sort of fits the situation but is not realistic, and not really helpful, it is worth 50 cents.

    -   If the thought has nothing to do with the situation and is not helpful, it is worth a penny.

5. Now take a look at the pesky thought your client tried to "pop" last week. How much is that thought worth? Create a chart listing all kinds of pesky and other thoughts and determine their worth together. Here is a chart you can use:

Thought:	How much is it worth?

Figure 55

6. Take a look at your client's thoughts together. Use a Socratic question to move her attention away from penny thoughts toward $100 thoughts. Wonder out loud something like this: *I am wondering why you are spending a lot of time and energy on a penny thought.*

7. Ask your client to elaborate on a $100 thought. This would be a thought that is realistic (does not have to be positive), fits the situation, and is helpful. Here is an example:

   > *I think I am running out of gas. I was not planning on it, but I think I am going to get gas. The gauge shows an empty tank, and I have 27 miles to go.*

   Ask your client why this is a $100 thought. The answer is simple: It will keep her out of trouble, it fits the situation and it is helpful. Even though it is not necessarily a pleasant thought, it is a thought that will drive her into behavior (getting gas) that will get her safely home.

8. Summarize what you have done so far: You have learned to differentiate between penny and $100 thoughts (and some in between). Penny thoughts are those that depression cons you into believing. They are not worth much, and once they are examined, their destructive nature becomes obvious.

9. Identify new homework: Use the "how much is it worth" thought chart to assign value to all kinds of thoughts. Give your client a blank copy of the chart and ask her to identify one thought per day and assign value to it. Explain that it would be best it if was a significant thought. Give her a copy of the chart to fill in.

	Thought:	How much is it worth?
Mon		
Tue		
Wed		
Thu		
Fri		
Sat		
Sun		

Figure 56

10. Closing. Check in with your client. Does she understand the purpose of assigning value to a thought? If this is difficult for her, you can change the assignment and simply ask her to rate a thought as helpful or not helpful. If you are working with a child, you can ask her to say "cha-ching" when she is having and identifying a $100 thought.

INTERVENTION 19

The Bully Thought

Some thoughts are worse than worthless because they tell your client that he should not be alive anymore. Even worse: The bully thought of needing to be dead may masquerade as a friendly thought, such as: "You deserve to be free of pain, and suicide is the best and only way to get there."

This intervention is for clients who struggle with bully thoughts about suicide and death. Once again, the key is to help your client take away the power of these thoughts in as many ways as possible.

Target skill: Defusion from bully thoughts. Recognition of relational connections that put bully thoughts in perspective.

1. Begin with empathy. Say clearly that you have noticed that your client's thoughts and feelings (and perhaps behaviors) have been focused more and more on death. Use your simple rating scale to gauge his depression. For a client with suicidal thoughts, it is very likely that he will gauge his depression as at least 8 (out of 10). Use the results of the scaling question as a doorway to talk with him about the need to address and contain suicidal thoughts (and, of course, behaviors).

2. Should you uncover suicidal thoughts, be sure to assess further for suicidal behaviors using a formal suicide risk assessment. If needed, create a safety plan and contact your supervisor. Follow your agency's protocol to assess the need for further and more intensive forms of intervention.

3. Let's assume you are working with a client who struggles with significant suicidal thoughts but does not have behaviors related to this. You must make a note that you need to assess for suicidal thoughts, means, and intent every time you see this client. Specifically ask about the things that your client is afraid to tell you. Ask: *What are you not telling me?* It is not unusual to uncover that a client has behaviors related to suicidal thoughts that he is afraid to disclose.

4. Once you have concluded that your client struggles with suicidal thoughts (or just generally has death on his mind), collaborate with him on identifying today's task: finding a way to manage those thoughts. What would this mean? How could this work? What has your client already tried?

5. Review last week's homework: Even though you are now dealing with a more serious situation (suicidal thoughts), you should still review last week's homework briefly. It is important to maintain the structure of your session. In addition, you can review how the idea of some thoughts having less value than others applies to suicidal thoughts. Was your client able to identify thoughts of value and thoughts of little value? What were they? Praise your client for being able to look at thoughts from afar and assign different values to them. If your client was not able to do this, this may already be an indicator that he is "fused" with his thoughts and struggles with evaluating evidence for and against the validity of the thought.

6. Work on today's task: taking a look at thoughts of death and suicide. You can get started by using the chart below. First, help your client name the bully thought. Then outline the evidence for and against the thought.

    Make a list with your client. Outline his specific thought of death and suicide. Name it a "bully thought" right away. You can go back to talking about depression as a great con man or liar. Depression tells you that you should and must die, but this is actually a lie.

Bully Thought: "I need to not be here. The world would be better off without me."
Evidence for:
• My kids tell me they hate me. • I have a lot of debt that I can never get rid of. • My partner left me.
Evidence against:
• My kids often say they need me and love me. • When I have a good day, there are things I enjoy such as . . . • My friends assure me that I am a great person to hang out with. • There are so many things I want to do.

Figure 57

7. Once your client has created the evidence list, take a good look at the "evidence for" with your client. Examine if the evidence for the validity of needing to be dead is actually evidence for something else. Be sure to do this in a kind manner. You are not devaluing your client's feelings. Wonder out loud: Does the fact that your client's partner left him really indicate that he should die? Ask Socratic questions about this. Here are some examples:

    - *Were you happy in the relationship?*

    - *Was your partner happy in the relationship?*

    - *Is it possible that you could have another relationship in time?*

    - *Are there things that worked in the relationship? What were they?*

    The key here is to examine the evidence and determine if it's just another bully thought.

8. Once you have examined the "evidence for" and viewed it in the context of the client's depression, help him expand the "evidence against" suicide/death. There is usually a lot more than your client can come up with. Think about all the names your client has mentioned in meetings. Each one of those names has potential to be on the list of evidence against.

    - Sue would miss me.

- Jay would miss me.

- The PTA would miss me.

- My children would miss me.

9. The aim here is not to make your client feel guilty about having thoughts of death and suicide, but rather to help him recognize all of the relational connections he has and the fact that he is contributing to the lives of others through his presence.

10. Expand the list of "evidence against" death/suicide as much as you can. When you are done it should be a lot longer than the list of "evidence for" death/suicide. Another way to expand the list is to have your client name all of the things he still wants to do. Where does he want to go? Who does he want to meet? If he could have any pet, what would it be? What kind of a house would he ideally want to live in? Help your client think beyond depression and the bully thought.

11. Review with your client what you have done so far: You have identified the bully thought. You have examined the evidence for and against the bully thought. You have looked at the bully thought in the context of depression lying to him. You uncovered that what seems like evidence for the bully thought is often just another lie depression tells. And you have greatly expanded on the evidence against suicide/death as a solution.

12. A deep depression can make it difficult to think. Homework for this session should take this into account. Send your client home with a completed list of evidence against the bully thought. You may want to give him two printed copies: one to carry around with him and one to hang over the kitchen sink. It is not necessary to name the bully thought on the assignment sheet. Your client already has the thought and does not need to be reminded. He needs to be reminded of his reasons to live and be with others. Here is a blank assignment sheet for you to give to your client:

Reasons to Be:
1.
2.
3.
4.
5.
6.
7.
8.
9.
10.

Figure 58

Be specific and clear. Ask him to go over the reasons every morning and every evening and whenever needed during the day.

13. Closing. Check in again with your client. Express empathy for the depth of his feelings. Acknowledge that thoughts of death can be difficult to carry around. Be sure to emphasize again that bully thoughts are not even worth a penny. Encourage your client to add to the list of "reasons to be."

INTERVENTION 20

Reasons to Be—For Me!

The last intervention focused mainly on helping your client recognize the connections she has and the relational reasons to stay in this life. It is often easier for those with suicidal thoughts to recognize that others may need them and depend on them than to assign value to their own being. The following intervention is focused on helping your client identify thoughts of who she is and who she wants to be, and assigning value to these thoughts.

Target skill: Self-compassion and self-worth. Finding meaning and joy.

1. Begin with empathy. During your last meeting you talked about your client's thoughts of suicide/death. Check in with your client. How is she feeling today? Help her gauge her feelings of depression using simple scaling questions. If her level of depression is still the same, reassure her that things can change, but change can take time. Help her be realistic about making change, and remind her that it's OK to need and ask for help with this.

2. Collaborate with your client on identifying today's task: recognizing the reasons your client wants to be here *for herself.* If she struggles with this, ask about her best friend. What is her best friend's name? What makes her such a good friend? What does she say? What does she do that makes her a good friend? Ask your client if her best friend deserves a good life. In all likelihood your client will say something like: "Well, yes, of course. She is a wonderful person."

3. Review last week's homework: Ask your client to take out the "reasons to be" list. Check to see if she added to it. Ask these kinds of questions:

   - *Did you take out the list at least daily?*

   - *What did you think when you read the list?*

   - *What did you feel?*

   Help your client acknowledge feelings of reluctance about using the list as well as feelings of commitment to her own life. Highlight those feelings of commitment and use language that helps your client recognize that even the smallest thoughts of self-worth are a great beginning.

4. Work on today's task: Use Socratic questions to help your client think about what her friend would say if the client shared her feelings about not deserving to be around. If your client struggles with this, role-play the situation. You will be the friend and your client will be herself. Here is what this role play could look like:

   Client: I am just a terrible person. I really shouldn't be here. I am just a burden for everyone.

   Friend: What? You are my best friend and I love having you around!

   Client: I think that I am just bothering you with all of my problems.

Friend: Oh, my goodness. You have helped me so much. I don't know what I would do without you. Do you remember when we __________?

Client: Yes, I do remember. I thought you went with me because you felt bad for me.

Friend: That's crazy. I went with you because we have such a good time together. You make my life better. And I do remember you having a good time. We were laughing so much.

Client: This is true. We did have a good time. I often think that I don't deserve to have a good time.

Friend: Not sure where that thought comes from, but that is just not true.

5. Now return to the task at hand: Identifying reasons why your client wants to be here for herself. Explain to your client that there is nothing wrong with doing things for herself just for the joy of doing them. Give examples:

   - *It's OK to ride a roller coaster, because it is fun.*
   - *It's OK to watch a comedy, because it is fun.*
   - *It's OK to think about wanting to travel.*
   - *It's OK to think about doing something good in the world. (Specify what this is).*
   - *It's OK to want to write a book, paint, dance.*

   Explain that before the action comes the thought. What kinds of thoughts about doing meaningful and joyful things are going through her mind? Help your client create a list. Every time one of depression's bully thoughts tells her that she should not think about doing joyful and meaningful things, help her to either tell the thought that it is a bully thought and "shush" it away, or acknowledge the thought but assign it a value of zero.

   Here is a template for the list:

I think the following things would give me joy:
I think the following things are meaningful to me:

Figure 59

Be sure to help your client identify at least three thoughts about what would give her joy and three thoughts about what would be meaningful to her.

6. While you are creating the list, pay attention to your client's affect and body language. If thinking about a specific activity animates your client, if you see the beginning of a smile, be sure to point this out. *It looks like you are on to something here. When you thought about horseback riding, your face lit up and you sat up. Tell me more!*

7. Then use Socratic questions to help your client think more about the activity that would give her joy or create meaning. In this manner you are "summoning" the feeling of the activity into the room (yes, you are venturing into working with the emotional component of the cognitive triangle for a moment). When you ask your client to elaborate about joy, you are actually creating it with her right there and then!

8. Summarize what you have done together so far: You have established that your client is deserving of joy and meaning and that she contributes to the lives of her friends and family because of who she is. You have asked your client to think about things that give her joy and are meaningful. You have brought the feeling of joy into the room as much as possible.

9. There are several possibilities for assigning homework related to today's work. You can move the homework over into the behavioral category and ask your client to pick three things from her list and do them over the course of the week. Mark those things on the list above and ask your client to place a check mark on them when they are completed.

    Your other option is to assign more thinking about joyful and meaningful things. You should do this if your client is not quite ready to try doing things. Send the above list home with your client to add to it. Ask her to identify at least two more things in each category over the course of the next week. If she wonders if she can do so, ask her to enlist the help of a friend or family member. She can ask her friend or family member what has brought her joy or meaning in the past, then have a conversation about this activity. If her friend or family member sees some excitement about the activity in your client's face, it should go on the list.

10. Closing. Check in with your client. Make sure she understands the assignment. Reiterate that your client deserves to think about and do things that give her joy and meaning. Leave your client with words of encouragement like these:

    - *Joy is contagious. The more joy you have, the more joy will grow.*

    - *Just start with allowing joy. You deserve it.*

    - *Don't worry about doing joy "right." Just recognize joy, when you experience it.*

INTERVENTION 21

Think Like a Wizard

This intervention continues the focus on building your client's capacity to think outside the box, to consider more things possible, to be more adventurous in the way he thinks. This intervention is well suited for the "Harry Potter generation." CBT generally promotes realistic thinking. How does thinking like a wizard fit with this? This intervention will help your client expand his thinking. Depression shuts doors and makes you think small. Thinking like a wizard opens doors in that it makes you think big. If your client thinks too big, you can always help him distill the essence of his big thoughts and move that essence into what is possible. For example: Your client really wants to be able to fly. Really. He does not mean fly in an airplane or a balloon. He really wants to be able to fly like a wizard using his magical powers.

Help him distill the essence of this using Socratic questions. What would it feel like to actually fly? Is he looking for adventure? Freedom? Does he want to feel more alive? Then help your client incorporate adventure and freedom into his life in realistic ways.

Target skill: Thinking outside the box (of depression). Thinking about the future. Daring to dream.

1. Begin with empathy. Check in with your client about his level of depression. Ask if he is beginning to see a difference in letting himself think more about things he likes/wants/can do. Help him elaborate on why. Reiterate that thinking can help him move into doing more things.

2. Collaborate with your client about identifying today's task: thinking like a wizard. If your client has a religious or other objection to thinking about wizardry, this intervention may not be for him. It may help to reiterate that you don't think wizardry is real, but that it may be helpful to pretend for a moment that it is. If your client is willing to go along with the intervention, ask him what it would be like to be a wizard. Listen to what he would do.

3. Review last week's homework: Was your client able to do three things that give him joy and meaning? If he did, what were they? Ask him to elaborate and watch for expressions of joy and meaning. Tell him what you see in his face and body language when he talks about the activities. If your client thought up more activities that could give him joy and meaning, help him elaborate on those, again paying attention to body language and facial expressions. Help him recognize any joy or hope you see in his face. If your client struggled with the assignment, find out why. Work with your client on removing barriers to homework completion.

4. Work with your client on thinking like a wizard. You can use the following worksheet to do so:

<table>
<tr><td>Thinking Like a Wizard</td></tr>
<tr><td>If I were a wizard I would have no trouble thinking about:

</td></tr>
<tr><td>If I were a wizard I would just:

</td></tr>
</table>

Figure 60

Here are some examples of what your client might fill in:

- Flying
- Going to Hawaii in a flash
- Teleporting wherever I want
- Turning into a frog

The second step simply translates thoughts into actions. So that may look like this:

- Fly
- Go to Hawaii
- Teleport to _________
- Turn ______ into a frog

A word about the use and abuse of wizard powers: You may think that it is not a good idea to dwell on the "turning someone into a frog" kind of activities. If these kinds of "punishments" are all your client comes up with, you may want to talk about the (imaginary, of course) wizard code of conduct. You can only use your wizard powers for the good of humanity. Temporary banishment of a difficult person into the frog world is permitted, but it must be reversed and the person must be unharmed.

5. Now help your client distill the essence of his thoughts. If he allows himself to think about wanting to fly with wizard powers, use Socratic questions to distill the essence of what your client is truly looking for. You can do this by asking questions like these: *If you could fly, what would this mean? If you could teleport anywhere, what would this mean for your life?*

6. Help your client identify the things he really wants and make a list of those things. Perhaps your client really wants to:

    - Feel free and be free.
    - Have more "lightness" in his life.
    - Have different kinds of relationships.

7. Summarize for and with your client what you have done so far: He has thought like a wizard. Ask him if this was fun! Elaborate with him on the fun. You have distilled from the wizard thoughts some things he really wants in his life. Name those things again.

8. Assign homework: Have the client identify next steps. You can use the following homework form to do so:

<table>
<tr><td>1.What I really want:

</td></tr>
<tr><td>Next steps:

</td></tr>
<tr><td>2. What I also really want:

</td></tr>
<tr><td>Next steps:

</td></tr>
<tr><td>3. Another thing I really want:

</td></tr>
<tr><td>Next steps:

</td></tr>
</table>

Figure 61

Ask your client to identify at least two things he really wants and to be concrete about next steps. If, for example, your client has identified that he would like to end a toxic relationship (turn someone into a frog), what would this mean in real life? Does he need to write a letter or make a phone call? Or does he first need to talk with a friend about the toxic relationship to clarify what he really wants?

9. Closing. Check in with your client to make sure he understands the assignment. Ask him if it was useful and fun to think like a wizard just for a minute. Make sure that he understands the assignment. If there are barriers, brainstorm with your client about removing them and write these plans on the homework sheet.

INTERVENTION 22

It's All Going to Pieces

This intervention is designed to help your client with a specific form of cognitive distortion, namely, thinking that the worst-case scenario is what is most likely to happen, or believing that it's the only thing that could ever happen. In CBT this kind of thinking is called catastrophizing.

Think of catastrophizing as a means of preparation for the worst-case scenario. If your client is always expecting the worst, then she won't be disappointed. Thinking that everything is falling to pieces is very common in people experiencing suicidal thoughts. Each catastrophizing thought reinforces the belief that life is not worth living; hence, catastrophizing thoughts must be addressed.

Target skill: Identifying and examining faulty thoughts and defusion from unhelpful thoughts.

1. Check in with your client about her level of depression. Has it changed since she started using the "think like a wizard" intervention? Has she gained some clarity about what she really needs and wants in her life? Is she able to expand her thinking, to think big thoughts about what she needs and wants?

2. Identify today's task: examining faulty thoughts about the odds of things going wrong. Give your client some examples of catastrophizing thoughts such as:

    - *No matter what I do, I can't succeed.*

    - *That mole means that I have cancer.*

    - *I will get fired. The only question is when.*

    Ask your client what she thinks about these statements. Do they ring true for her? Does she recognize them?

3. Check in with your client about the homework. Was your client able to identify two things she really wants and next steps to get to them? If she was not able to, then identify the next steps. Reinforce that once your client can identify what she wants, she can learn how to get there. It may take time, but as long as the goal is realistic and achievable, reassure her that you can work on her goals together. If necessary, help her set more realistic and achievable goals. Explain that while it is not impossible for your client to own a mansion in the future, having stable and safe housing is a realistic goal that could impact her mental health in positive ways.

4. Work with your client on today's task: identifying "going to pieces" thinking. Help your client create a list of her catastrophizing thoughts. Here is a form you can use:

"Going to pieces" thought:	Evidence for the thought:	Evidence against the thought:

Figure 62

Begin by collecting the thoughts and writing them down. If there are specific themes, help your client identify them. Is her catastrophizing centered on finances or relationships?

5. Normalize the presence of "going to pieces" thinking. Also explain that just because your client is having a catastrophizing thought, this does not mean that the thought is true. Remind her that a thought is just a thought.

6. Reintroduce the idea that thoughts can be examined. Explain that a thought can be realistic and appropriate for the situation or unrealistic.

7. In addition, explore the idea that catastrophizing thoughts can be another way that depression is lying to her. Catastrophizing thoughts are depression-maintaining thoughts.

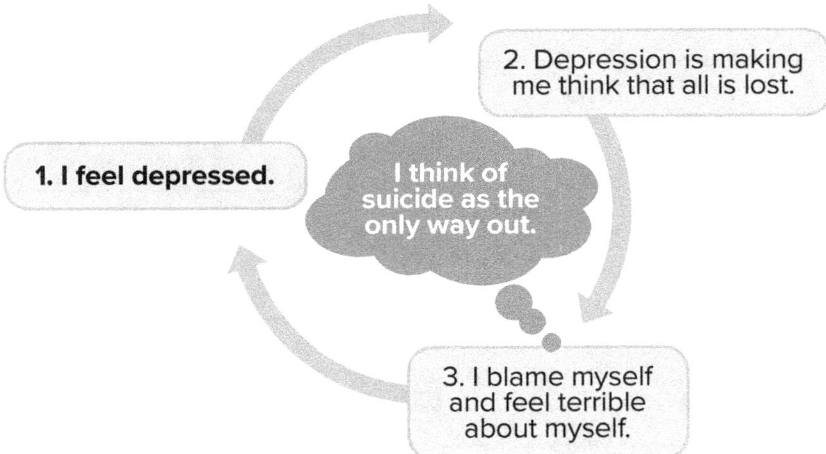

Figure 63

8. Explain that there is a way out of the depression-maintaining thinking, which is examining thoughts for their truthfulness.

9. Go back to your client's "going to pieces" chart. Ask your client to pick one thought, perhaps the one that comes to her most often. Examine this thought together. It may be easiest to pull that one thought from the chart and create a new one:

"Going to pieces" thought:	
Evidence for the thought:	
Evidence against the thought:	

Figure 64

You can see where this is going. There is a lot more space in the "evidence against the thought" part of the chart, simply because it is unlikely that there is much evidence for the catastrophic thought. Perhaps your client has a mole and thinks that the only explanation is that she has incurable skin cancer. What is the evidence for this? Really only the fact that your client has a mole and sometimes a mole can be identified as cancerous. That's it.

The evidence against the thought is much more plentiful and sound. Most moles are not cancerous (you could look up a percentage if this is helpful). The shape of the mole points to it just being a mole. The mole has been there for many years, your client is just now paying attention to it. Her mother has the same mole, and so on. In the case of a mole, your client could really benefit from seeing a doctor.

Ask her to think about the possibility that the mole is just a mole. What would this mean for her life? If the mole is just a mole, are there other thoughts where your client is making a mountain out of a molehill (pun intended)?

10. Your client may be reluctant to adjust her thinking based on examining the evidence. That is to be expected. Explain that "going to pieces" thinking is a habit that depression has pushed on her, and that all you are asking her to do at this point is to *consider* that the thought is not valid.

11. Summarize with and for your client what you have done together so far: She has identified a few of her "going to pieces" thoughts. You have gone back to reminding her that a thought can be examined for its truthfulness. You have examined one of her thoughts together, and she has agreed to consider the possibility that it's not valid.

12. Identify new homework. Ask your client to ask herself how her life would be different if her catastrophizing thought was not true. Would she view herself differently? How about the world? Or friends? Give your client an index card and ask her to take notes and bring it to the next meeting. Here is a card you could use:

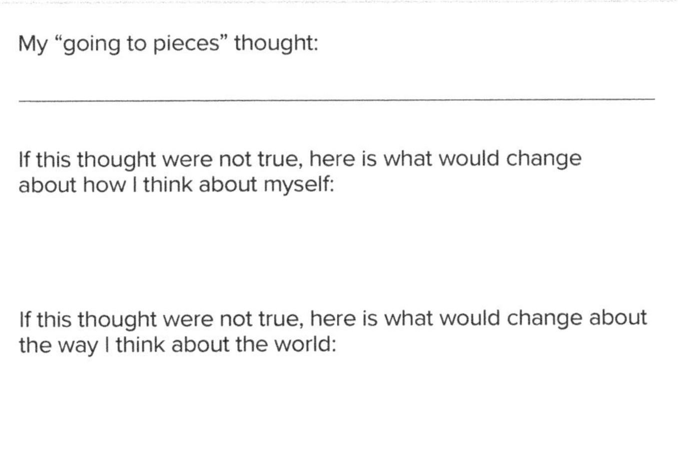

Figure 65

13. Closing. Check in with your client. How does she feel about the possibility that her "going to pieces" thoughts might be lying to her? Can she consider the possibility? Is she willing to consider that there might be a better and more realistic way of thinking? Encourage her to explore this possibility over the next week.

Going to Pieces and Being OK

This intervention addresses a cognitive error: Namely that we should always be OK and things should not ever feel like they are falling apart. Yet "going to pieces" and then putting oneself back together is really a part of life. Things don't always go our way. We can feel fragile. In fact, the process of "going to pieces" can be a call to action. Something may not be right, and we need to address it. "Going to pieces" can be a chance to be truly human, acknowledge the fragility of life, and then put the pieces of the puzzle back together in a way that works for right now.

Target skill: Acceptance. Openness to change.

1. Check in with your client about his level of depression using simple scaling questions. If your client's level of depression is decreasing, make a note of this with him. If your client's level of depression remains the same but his ability to manage his depression is increasing, also make a note of it. You may want to begin using a scale for this client that measures his ability to manage his depression. Here is a sample scale you can use:

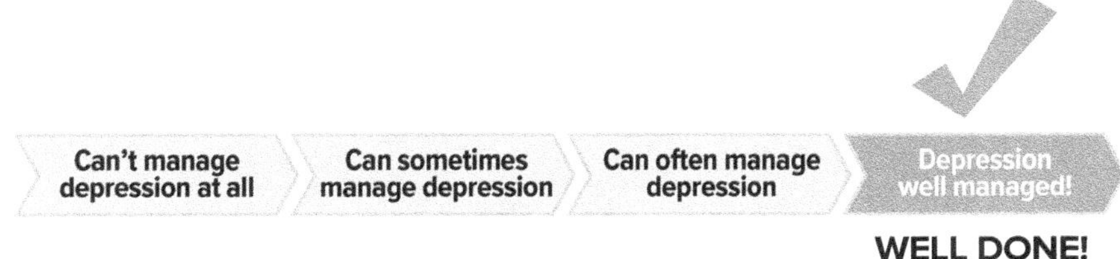

Figure 66

    Work with your client on recognizing the importance of managing his depression. Managing depression does not mean giving up on leaving depression behind. It means setting a realistic goal for the time being.

2. Collaborate with your client on identifying today's task: accepting that sometimes things are falling apart and that this is OK. Things are not always perfect and there will be periods of turmoil in life resulting in changes. Ask your client about his response to this statement.

3. Review last week's homework: Was your client able to think about his "going to pieces" thought? Was he able to consider that it might not be true? Was he able to think about how his life would change if his thought were not true? Keep in mind that the underlying purpose of the assignment is to help your client recognize that a thought is just a thought and that thoughts can be examined.

If it is appropriate for your client, you can point out the tension between last week's work—disproving the thought that things are going to pieces—and this week's work, accepting that things sometimes go to pieces. Explain to your client that these are just different ways of looking at thoughts and that it is OK to look at a thought in more than one way.

4. Work with your client on today's task: accepting that sometimes things go to pieces and that this is OK. You may want to show your client the following image and say:

> *Things are going to pieces.*
>
> *Things are falling apart.*
>
> *It's time for a new start:*
>
> *Rearrange the pieces*
>
> *Piece by piece,*
>
> *Building a life that works.*

Figure 67

5. Ask your client to identify the pieces of his life. They can be pieces that seem broken right now (perhaps a relationship) and pieces that work for him (perhaps his relationship with his child). In the process you can also ask your client to identify missing puzzle pieces. Here is a chart that can help with this:

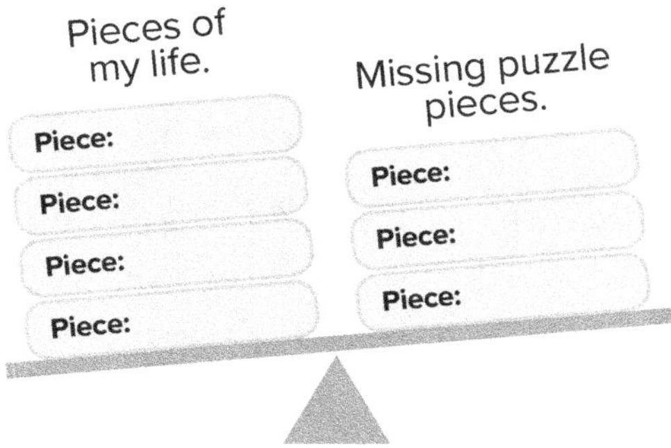

Figure 68

You can see that things are kind of "wobbly" and off kilter here. Sometimes life just is that way. Feel free to add a lot more pieces. Get a larger piece of paper. If your client struggles with identifying the pieces of his life, ask him about his past and his future.

6. Once you have collected the pieces of your client's life with him (including missing pieces), help him think about rearranging them. Your client may want to cut out those pieces and rearrange them on a new piece of paper (provide glue). It is quite possible that your client may want to get rid of a piece. This is OK.

7. Reiterate that the thought "things are going to pieces" can be an opportunity to examine life as it is right now and rearrange the pieces. Your client can add missing pieces to his life and discard pieces that no longer fit.

8. Emphasize that change is an ongoing process and takes time. Missing puzzle pieces sometimes take a while to find. This is OK. And it can be difficult to discard pieces that no longer fit. This is OK, too.

9. Summarize with and for your client what you have done so far: You have explored the idea that sometimes things go to pieces and that this can be a part of life. Your client has identified the pieces of his life, including missing pieces. He has rearranged the pieces in a way that works for him right now. Your client understands that change can take time and that is OK.

10. Assign new homework: Ask your client to identify three categories of puzzle pieces in his life—pieces he has, pieces that are missing, and pieces he needs to discard—and make a note of them on this chart, then bring the chart back for your next meeting:

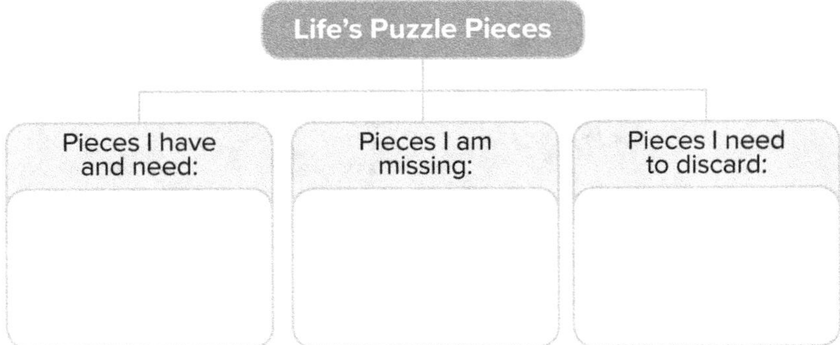

Figure 69

11. Closing. Check in with your client. What is it like for him to consider that sometimes things fall apart and that this is OK? Does he understand the homework? If you need to, provide him with examples for all three kinds of puzzle pieces.

INTERVENTION 24

It's Not Fair

Fairness is one of the things in life we all want. This includes our clients. Fairness is a good thing. It helps us feel more secure and less anxious. When things are fair, we know what to expect. But we all come to experience the fact that life is not always fair. Most of our clients would say it is not fair that they have to struggle with depression. This is surely true. It is simply not fair. Having a learning disability is not fair. There are lots of other examples. This intervention is designed to help your client move on from the thought that life should be fair, without giving up the idea that fairness is a good thing worth fighting for.

Target skill: Acceptance. Value identification. Taking action.

1. Check in with your client about her level of depression and her ability to manage her depression using a simple scale. Ask:

    What are you doing differently this week to manage your depression? What kinds of thoughts are you thinking? Are you able to examine your thoughts?

2. Collaborate with your client on identifying today's task: finding a way of accepting that life can be less than fair while honoring the idea that fairness is worth fighting for. Ask your client to elaborate on her idea of fairness.

3. Review last week's homework with your client: Was she able to identify different kinds of puzzle pieces in her life? Take a look at the pieces she is missing and the pieces she wants to discard. Through this process help her accept that sometimes it's OK to rearrange pieces of one's life.

4. Work with your client on today's task: accepting that life is not always fair, even though fairness is worth fighting for. Begin by asking: How would your life be different if things were fair? Help her create a list using the following chart:

If life was fair I . . .
1.
2.
3.
4.
5.
6.

Figure 70

5. Once your client has completed the chart, take a look at it together. Perhaps there are many things on this list your client wants. They could be relational or material wishes.

6. Compliment your client on knowing what she wants. Then ask her: If life never became fair, would she just give up on these things? Or would she still want them?

7. Explore with your client how she would want to spend her energy:

   - Would she want to spend her energy being angry about the fact that life is not fair?

   - Or would she want to spend her energy going after the things she wants in life in spite of the fact that life is not fair?

8. Explain that the second way of thinking about fairness gives her a chance to get the things she wants, while the first does not. Help your client elaborate on this. Perhaps she thinks it is unfair that she never has any money to spend. What are her choices? She could be angry about not having money and still have no money, or she could look for a better job or learn a new set of skills that lead to a better-paying job. Only the latter will actually get her where she wants to be.

9. Your client may have some objections here. She may say, "But things should be fair. We need to build a world in which things are fair." I would agree with her on this. She may want to join a movement that advocates for a fairer world. That is a good way to spend her energy. In the meantime, while the world is not yet fair, she can also find ways of getting what she wants in life.

10. It may be helpful to explain to your client the difference between accepting that life is not fair and endorsing the idea that life should not be fair. Acceptance is a good thing. Endorsing the idea that life should be unfair is not.

11. Summarize today's work: You have examined the idea of fairness. You have used the idea of fairness to help your client identify the things she really wants in life (the things she would have if life were fair). You have encouraged your client to accept the thought that life can be unfair at times, but that this should not stop her from going after the things she wants. In other words: You have asked your client to think realistically about life.

12. Assign homework: Send your client home with an index card that looks like this:

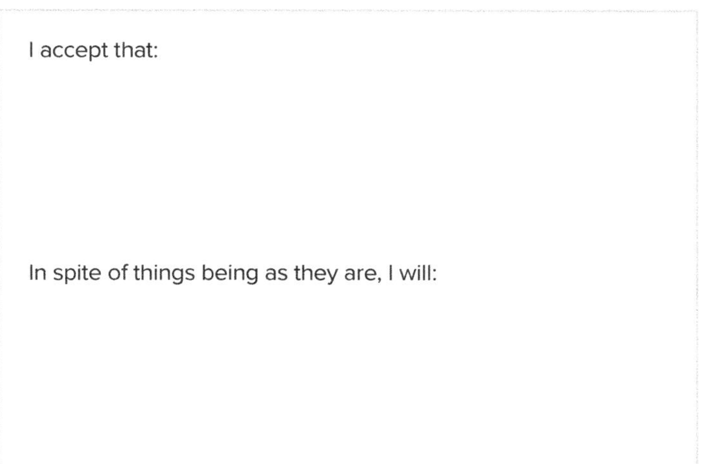

Figure 71

Ask your client to use this card every time she is upset with something that seems unfair (this is the "I accept that . . ." part). Then ask her to write down action steps she can take despite things not being fair.

13. Closing. Check in with your client. How does she feel about this new way of thinking about fairness? Is it a difficult thing for her to accept that things can be unfair? If it is, reassure her that most people would agree with her on this. Explain that you don't want her to get stuck because life is treating her unfairly, that you want her to get as close as she can to the life she wants, and that this can only happen if she takes active steps toward her goals despite unfairness.

I Think the World Is Out to Get Me

Imagine that you walk into the kitchen at your workplace and everyone falls silent. There could be many reasons for this, but it can be easy to think like this:

- They were talking about me.
- They do not like me.
- They are excluding me from ________.
- They are conspiring to get me fired.

Here is the mechanism at work: I do not know what is really going on. I personalize the situation and think that whatever my colleagues are doing, it must be about me and it is probably about me in the worst possible way.

There are, of course, many alternative ways of thinking about this situation:

- It's just a coincidence.
- They are planning my birthday party.
- They need to get back to work.

This intervention is designed to help your client step back from the thought that whatever is happening is probably about him and move toward exploring alternative explanations.

Target skill: Identifying thought errors. Defusion. Adaptive and realistic thinking.

1. Check in with your client. Help him gauge his level of depression and his ability to manage his depression using simple scaling questions. Ask your client what went well over the past week. If something went well, ask your client what he did differently, and how that helped. Did he think differently or act differently? How did his thinking or acting differently make a difference no matter how small?

2. Introduce your client to today's task: finding alternative ways of thinking when taking things too personally. Ask your client if he has ever taken things too personally. Perhaps this has happened at work. Or perhaps this has happened even in the helping relationship between you and him.

3. Review last week's homework: Was your client able to list specific situations or conditions he has to accept in spite of their being unfair? Was your client able to take some action steps toward the things he wants? If this was difficult for him, this is OK. Explain that most people struggle with the idea that things are not always fair. Also explain again that it is possible to take action steps toward life goals in spite of things not being fair.

4. Work on today's task: finding alternative ways of thinking when taking things too personally. Tell your client the following story:

Ted was having a very bad day. When he was fixing his coffee in the morning he noticed that he was out of his favorite creamer. Then, when he jumped in the car, he noticed that he was low on gas. Now he had to stop and get gas, which would make him late. On the way to work things got worse: Someone rear-ended his car. His new car. Ted was getting upset. He had to wait for police to come and file a report. The accident was not even his fault, but he was now running extremely late. He walked into the office with a frown on his face. On his way into the office he passed his secretary. He did not even look at her.

Now Ted's secretary was worried. She did not know about Ted's tough morning. She worried about having forgotten something. She worried about having said the wrong thing to Ted yesterday. She worried that she might get fired for having done something wrong.

5. Ask your client how he could help Ted's secretary. What information is Ted's secretary missing? What would your client say to Ted's secretary to help her understand that whatever is going on has nothing to do with her?

6. Ask your client to find a name for Ted's secretary's thinking error. If your client struggles with this, explore together some of the things Ted's secretary might be thinking :

   - "Whatever it is, it has something to do with me."
   - "Whatever it is, it is probably my fault."
   - "I am responsible for Ted having a good day."
   - "I should always understand Ted."

7. You can also use this image to help your client understand what is wrong with Ted's secretary's thinking:

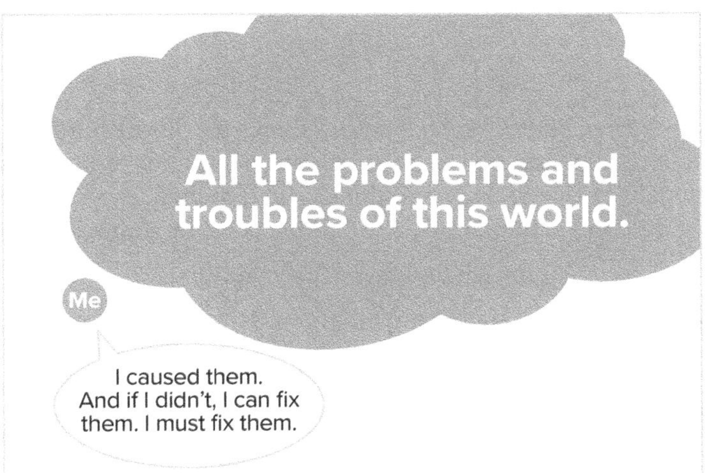

Figure 72

Clearly, it is impossible that one person is responsible for so many problems and troubles. It is also unrealistic to for Ted's secretary to expect to know what is really going on and for him to expect to fix things.

8. If it helps your client, you can name this kind of thinking "personalizing," meaning that everything that happens somehow relates to me, is caused by me, or needs to be fixed by me.

9. Explain that this kind of thinking maintains depression because it's not realistic. We can't read each other's minds or be responsible for everything that happens around us. Here is how personalizing things maintains depression:

I see a problem.
I think it is mine to solve.

But it's not actually my problem.
It's not about me!

I feel terrible because
I can't fix the situation.

Figure 73

10. Ask your client if he ever personalizes things that have nothing to do with him. If he does, explore examples of how he responds to situations that he personalizes. Use Socratic questions to help your client recognize how damaging this kind of thinking can be for him. Here are some sample questions:

- When you think it is about you, how do you feel?

- When you can't figure out how to fix the situation, how do you feel?

- How could you change your thinking about the situation?

- How do you think you would feel if you changed your thinking?

11. Summarize what you have done together so far: You have shared a story about Ted, whose secretary misinterprets what is really going on and thinks she has done something wrong. You have given this kind of thinking a name:

Personalizing. If your client prefers to name it differently, this is OK. You have examined how personalizing thoughts misinterpret situations and can maintain depression.

12. Assign homework. Give your client a checklist to use during the week to help him stay away from personalizing thoughts. Ask him to use the checklist to avoid falling into the trap of trying to fix other people's problems or be involved in situations that have nothing to do with him. Here is a sample checklist to use:

Is this about me?
Did I cause the situation?
Is it for me to try to resolve the situation?
If I did not cause the situation and it is not for me to resolve it: **I stay away from it. I move on.**

Figure 74

It is a good idea to explain to your client that it may take some time to step away from situations he did not cause if this has been a habit.

13. Closing. Check in with your client. How does he feel about letting go of situations? Explain again that not personalizing situations will help him feel less depressed. Leave your client with words of encouragement like these:

- *It can be tough to let go of the need to fix everything.*
- *But it can be done.*
- *Not everything is your responsibility.*
- *The more you let go of trying to fix everything, the better you will feel.*

INTERVENTION 26

Living Your Own Life—Letting Go of "Should"

It's easy to not live your own life. All you have to do is listen to what others tell you to do. There is usually plenty of advice around. It is also not unusual to find that it is impossible to do everything the way you "should" do it. There are so many different circumstances. Clearly your circumstances are different from those of your parents. Hence, what you "should" do is probably different from what your parents "should" do. What can be done is dependent on the situation and who is involved.

This is not to say that one should abandon all rules. Clearly, there are some basic rules that make it possible for humans to get along. But when it comes to specific situations, it is often better to think about what you want out of the situation and how you can get there.

Target skill: Identifying and letting go of unhelpful thoughts. Adaptive and realistic thinking.

1. Check in with your client and help her gauge her current level of depression or ability to manage depression. Ask her what went well in the last few days. Is she able to examine her thoughts? Do things differently? Ask for specific examples.

2. Introduce your client to today's task: stepping away from burdening oneself with "should" thinking and using situation- and person-specific thinking to make decisions. Ask your client if she can name situations in which she felt burdened by thinking: "I should be doing ________."

3. Review last week's homework: Was your client able to use the "Is this about me?" checklist? How did using the checklist affect her? Was she able to step away from some situations? How did it feel? Encourage your client to continue to assess her involvement in situations that she did not cause and can't resolve. Explain again that stepping away from those situations can decrease feelings of depression.

4. Work on today's task: letting go of "should" thoughts that increase depression and focusing on the specific situation and her values. Ask your client the things she thinks she should do and make a list of those things. Here is a form you can use for this:

I should:

Figure 75

There are all kinds of things that could go on this list. Here is a list of things you may encounter:

- I should be nice to people.

- I should eat well.

- I should not smoke.

- I should do all of my homework right after school.

- I should eat breakfast.

5. Ask your client how she feels when she uses the word "should." Is there a quality of coercion? Once she decides she "should" do something, does it seem more likely she will do it? Or does the word "should" build a barrier between herself and the thing that "should" be done?

6. Suggest that your client pick the most important thing from her "I should" list. If she has trouble choosing, it's OK to pick more than one thing. Now ask her to replace the "should" with "I really want to." You may end up with something like this: "I really want to quit smoking."

7. Explain that she has just transformed an obligation into a personal goal. She has removed the barrier of "should" (meaning someone else thinks she should do it) and moved to a more authentic personal goal based on her personal values.

8. Ask your client how her relationship to her thought changed when she moved from "I should" to "I really want to." If this does not feel right, then the obligation will not transform into a personal goal. Here is an example:

Obligation: "I should always be nice to everyone."

Personal goal: "I really want to always be nice to everyone."

If the latter does not ring true (most of us do not really want to always be nice to everyone), then there is a good chance that it is an unreasonable obligation.

9. Summarize with and for your client what you have done so far: You have created a list of things your client feels she should do. Your client has picked the most important thing from the list if things she "should" do and has changed the language (and hence her thinking) to "I really want to _______."

10. You have examined together how changing the language affects your client's relationship with a thought.

11. Identify homework: Give your client the following index card to carry around with her and take a look at every time she feels she "should" do something:

Figure 76

Explain that if your client feels burdened by a self-imposed "I should," she can take a look at the index card. If she is able to complete the sentence "I really want to," then the situation or issue is likely truly important to her and related to her living a value-based life. If she can't, it is likely that the situation is not really important to her at this time.

Explain that there are, of course, many things we "should" do, such as brush our teeth after every meal. In a sense, this intervention is also about letting go of perfectionism.

12. Closing. Check in with your client. How does she feel about letting go of a few "shoulds"? If your client struggles with this, tell her that this is OK. It will take time to think differently. Explain that once again you are working on changing thinking, and that she has a choice in how she relates to her thoughts. They can be "should" thoughts or "I really want to" thoughts.

I Really Don't *Know!*

This intervention focuses on changing the kind of thinking that creates a lot of suffering in our clients' lives, namely, thinking that we know what a person is thinking or what her intentions are when we really do now know. We make assumptions about other people's intentions and desires. Even well-attuned people make mistakes with these kinds of assumptions. Even well-attuned people do better when they ask: What are you thinking? What do you want?

This kind of attempted mind reading maintains depression. When we get things wrong, we blame ourselves, thinking, "I should have known."

The following intervention is designed to help your client develop a sense of curious inquiry. Anytime your client finds herself making assumptions or trying to read someone else's mind, she learns to instead take a step back and say to herself: "I really don't know. But I can find out."

Target skill: Evaluating assumptions. Communication. Adaptive and realistic thinking.

1. Check in with your client about her current level of depression or her ability to manage her depressing using simple scaling questions. Ask her about what worked in the past week. Was she able to think or act differently? Always focus on what she was able to do and help her recognize any progress, no matter how small.

2. Collaborate with your client on identifying today's task: moving away from making assumptions about what goes on in other people's minds, and asking questions instead. Ask your client if she ever makes assumptions about what another person is thinking. You may also want to give an example like this:

    > *Joey is done with his class work. He thinks that his teacher would probably want him to just start the next chapter in the book, so he goes ahead and gets a head start on the next chapter. Before he knows it, his teacher walks by and scolds him for working ahead. Joey is now upset with himself for making a mistake.*

3. Review last week's homework with your client: Was your client able to move from "I should" to "I really want to" thinking? What does it feel like to make this switch? Does she feel more in control of her choices? If it was hard to think differently, this is OK. Learning to think differently can be difficult at first.

4. Work on today's task: Ask your client about her experiences with trying to read someone else's mind. When working with an adult, it is often easiest to talk about close relationships. Ask questions like these:

    - *Do you ever try to please your mother by guessing what she wants? Does this always work out well?*

- *Do you ever try to guess what your partner wants? Perhaps you got him the gift you were sure he wanted and then saw a look of disappointment on his face?*

- *Do you ever try to read your supervisor's mind? Are you always right about what you think he is thinking?*

5. If this is difficult for your client, you can use your relationship with her as an example. You can ask your client if she ever thinks she knows what you are thinking or want her to do. Sometimes clients can be sure that we "hate" them, because they misread situations. This is especially true when a client is struggling with depression. Depression can con your client into making faulty and negative assumptions about what you think of her. If your client is able, ask her to do some fact checking with you.

   - First, ask your client to write down three things that she thinks you think about her.

   - Then encourage your client to ask you questions related to those things to determine if she was right or wrong.

   Here are some questions a client may ask:

   - *Do you think I am a lost cause?*

   - *Do you think I should have gotten this by now?*

   - *Do you think that I am lazy because I often don't do my homework?*

6. Carefully answer your client's questions with kindness. If your client got something right, this is great. But overall, emphasize that we can't really know what another person is thinking or wants us to do until we ask.

7. You can use the following image to help your client understand what can go wrong when we make assumptions:

ASSUMPTION:
Jack wants me to do the laundry
because I see it piled in front of the washer.

ACTION:
I do the laundry.

PROBLEM:
Jack wanted to sort the laundry when he got home.
Colors are all mixed. Jack is upset with me.

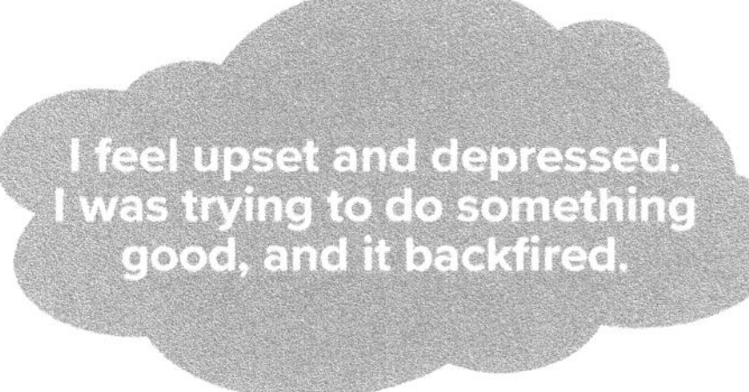

Figure 77

8. Role-play with your client what she could have done instead. She will be herself. You will be Jack. Before your role play, help your client identify questions she could ask Jack, such as:

   - Is there a reason you put the laundry in front of the washer?

   - Do you need help with the laundry?

   - How can I be helpful with the laundry?

   - Do you want help with the laundry or do you want me to leave it?

9. Reflect on your role play together. What is it like not to make assumptions? Is it easy for her to ask questions? Or is it difficult?

10. Ask your client to elaborate on what problems she avoided by asking clear questions. Then ask her how avoiding those problems may impact the way she feels.

11. Now turn the tables. Ask your client how she would like people to approach her. Does she want them to make assumptions and try to read her mind? Or does she want them to simply ask what she is thinking and what she wants?

12. Keep in mind that many people, especially women, have been taught that they should anticipate other people's needs. You can explain that this contributes greatly to feelings of depression. If you are asked to do something

that is impossible, you can only lose. This is why you are helping your client move away from making assumptions and toward asking questions.

13. Summarize with and for your client what you have done so far: You have examined how difficult it is to read someone's mind. You have determined that trying to do so will likely cause your client suffering. You have built inquisitive curiosity skills.

14. Give your client the following slogan to carry around (perhaps on an index card):

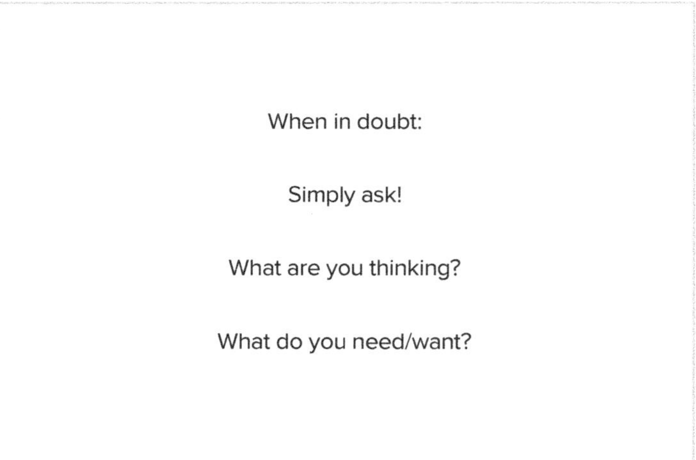

Figure 78

15. Assign homework: Ask your client to carry this card with her and use it every time she finds herself making assumptions or trying to guess what someone else is thinking or wants her to do. Suggest that she keep a record of her assumptions on the back of the index card and make a brief note about how things worked out differently by asking questions.

16. Closing. Check in with your client. Does she understand what it means to make assumptions or try to read someone else's mind? Is she willing to try to ask questions? If this is difficult for her, simply explore with her how she would like others to treat her. Does she want them to guess and get it wrong? Or does she want them to ask her questions and get it right? Explain that it is OK not to know what another person thinks or wants. It's OK to ask!

A Little Help from My Friends

Sometimes it can be difficult to evaluate thoughts. If your client has thought one way for a long time, distorted thinking may have become a habit, like eating too much candy. And habits can be difficult to break. In this intervention, you are asking your client to enlist the help of his best friends to break the habit of faulty thinking.

Target skill: Asking for help. Communication. Evaluating thoughts.

1. Check in with your client about his current level of depression or ability to manage depression. Ask your client what went well over the past week. You can also ask what did not go well, as this may help you assess for distorted thinking.

2. Collaborate with your client on identifying today's task: Be empathetic. Explain that you understand how difficult it can be to break the habit of faulty thinking. Explain that it is good to have backup and that today you would like him to build a support team to help him challenge and change distorted thinking that is harmful to him.

3. Review last week's homework: What was it like to ask questions instead of making assumptions? Was your client able to avoid some disappointments and misunderstandings by simply asking questions? Were there any changes in how your client felt when he made decisions based on questions and answers instead of assumptions? How comfortable is your client with asking questions? Explain that asking questions instead of making assumptions is a habit that can be learned.

4. Work with your client on today's task: Checking in about the reality and validity of pesky thoughts with his best friends. Explain to your client that some thoughts can be so pesky, he needs a team to question them and "shush" them away. Begin by establishing your client's team. Here is a simple way you can do so:

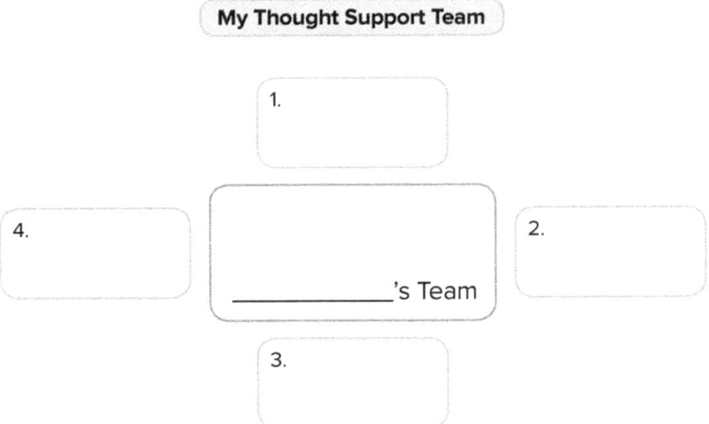

Figure 79

Keep in mind that it is not important that there are a lot of friends on the team, but rather that your client chooses supportive and kind friends or family members. People who want him to do well. If your client wants he can use photos or drawings to illustrate the support-team image.

5. Once you have established who should be on the team, ask your client to pick a particularly pesky automatic thought and write it down. As always, if your client struggles with writing, you can be his scribe. You can also decorate the support team chart with stickers or drawings!

   Now you can work with your client on how his support team would respond to his pesky automatic thought. You can do this by using the following chart:

PESKY AUTOMATIC THOUGHT:

What _________________ would say about this:

How I would feel if I believed this:

What _________________ would say about this:

How I would feel if I believed this:

What _________________ would say about this:

How I would feel if I believed this:

Figure 80

6. Encourage your client to listen to the other voices in his life: the voices of his friends and family, those who love and support him the most.

7. Explain that it may be good to keep the record of what his friends would say about his pesky automatic thought handy when negative thoughts about himself, others, and the world bombard him.

8. Explain that in particularly challenging times (if your client struggles with suicidal thoughts), it is a good idea to actually call on the members of his support team to support him in person. It is much harder to dismiss what a good friend says to your face than something written on paper.

9. Summarize with and for your client what you have done so far: You have explored the need for a thought support team to address faulty negative thinking. You have "assembled" the team on paper and explored how the team would respond to your client's most pesky thought. You have also established that when your client has a very distressing pesky thought (such as a suicidal thought), he may want to arrange to see his support team (or part of it) face to face.

10. Identify homework: In order for the thought support team to work, your client needs to "appoint" only supportive people to the team. And team members need to agree to be available, if possible, when called upon. Ask your client to make phone calls to the people he has named and ask them if they could be available by phone or in person when needed.

11. If your client says that he has absolutely no one to support him, you will need to work with him on building a supportive social network. It is also possible that your client does not see who is supportive of him due to his depression. In the latter case, you would need to help your client recognize and use the supports he has, even if they are imperfect.

12. Closing. Check in with your client: What does he think about establishing a thought support team? How attached is he to his habitual faulty thoughts? Challenge him to mindfully listen to each member of his support team and consider the possibility that his best friends may just be right.

So I'm Just a Bad Thinker?

Because depression produces many self-defeating thoughts, it is important for your client to understand the difference between labeling a thought as unhelpful or unrealistic, and thinking of oneself as a "bad thinker." Everyone has unhelpful thoughts. This intervention will help your client normalize and accept this.

Target skill: Acceptance. Identification of cognitive errors. Self-compassion.

1. Check in with your client about her current level of depression or ability to manage her depression. Are things moving in the right direction? If they are, what is she doing and how is she changing her thinking? If things are not moving in the right direction, provide support and encouragement. Explain that it can take a while to get a grip on the depression, and that this does not mean that she is not working hard or that there is something fundamentally wrong with her.

   If your client is suffering from a persistent depression what will not lift or is constantly battered by suicidal thoughts and intrusive thoughts about suicidal actions, discuss the need to refer her for a psychiatric consultation. Sometimes depression can be so persistent and intrusive that your client becomes unable to examine her thoughts and actions, and in this case a psychiatrist should decide whether medication is indicated.

2. Collaborate with your client on identifying today's task: making sure your client understands that labeling thoughts as pesky or distorted does not mean that she is a bad thinker. This is why we don't call distorted thoughts "bad" thoughts—they are just thoughts. Ask your client how she feels when you talk about distorted thinking. If she feels invalidated, help her understand that she can examine thoughts and their validity. And if she finds that her thoughts are unrealistic and do not fit a situation, she can determine what thoughts are distorted.

   If there is a need, you and your client can explore how her difficult life experiences have changed her thinking. If she expects only to be hurt in relationships, this is understandable. She has adjusted her expectations to "fit" her past experiences. But does this truly mean that nothing good can come of relationships? That all people are bad? Help your client understand that it is possible to change thinking that is based on past hurt. This is also a good time to talk about realistic thinking versus positive thinking. Positive thinking can be distorted thinking! CBT does not advocate for positive thinking, because things do not always go well.

3. Review last week's homework: Was your client able to solidify her thought support team? How did her friends respond to being asked to be on the team? Has she used the team yet? Reiterate the importance of using the support team when challenging thoughts come along.

4. Work with your client on today's task: Explore with your client what she thinks it means that she is able to think distorted and challenging thoughts.

Listen carefully. Is your client blaming herself for distorted and challenging thoughts? Does she think that she is a little bit crazy for having those kinds of thoughts?

5. Revisit the idea that the brain is able to generate thousands of thoughts in a very short time, that thoughts can be triggered by anything—a smell, a memory, an image, a bodily sensation. Having all kinds of thoughts about all kinds of things is in no way strange. It is how our brains function. Here is an image that may help your client understand:

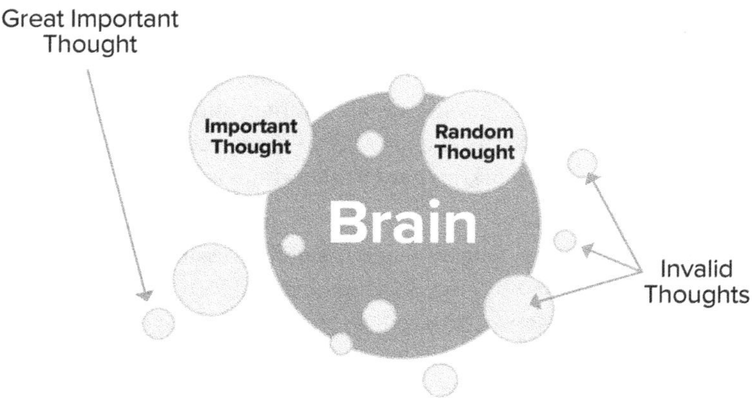

Figure 81

6. As your client can see, it is not always clear what thought is important, realistic, and valid. A great important thought may be in the back of your mind. A random thought can take up a lot of our thinking space.

7. Ask your client to create her own image of thoughts in her brain, once again reinforcing the idea that thoughts can be observed and examined for their validity and truthfulness.

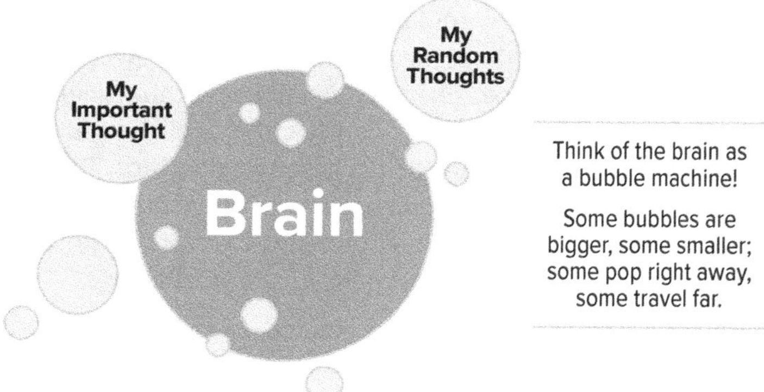

Figure 82

Help your client identify and find a place for her very important thought, the one that is really important but is sort of hiding from her. Encourage your client to become a scientist examining her own thoughts. If you are working with a child, you could give her a lab coat (easy to make out of an oversized white T-shirt cut open in the front) to reinforce the idea that she is a scientist.

8. Look at your client's illustration of her brain and thoughts together. Normalize the idea of the brain producing all kinds of thoughts, distorted or otherwise. Say:

    You are not a bad thinker. You are a normal thinker. This is what brains do. As humans we get to be scientists about our thoughts, we get to sort them and link them with reality. We get to discard unrealistic and unhelpful thoughts. This is great news.

9. Elaborate with your client on the idea of symbolically discarding distorted thoughts by putting them into the trash.

10. Summarize with your client what you have done together so far: You have examined how brains work. Your client has taken a look at the kinds of thoughts her brain produces. You have determined that having distorted thoughts is normal and that humans have the ability to disregard distorted thoughts.

11. Assign homework: Ask your client to take 5 minutes at the end of each day and make a list of some of the thoughts she recalls on a simple piece of paper. Any thoughts—realistic, distorted, and random. Explain that you will take a look at the list of thoughts together during your next meeting to continue with your scientific exploration of thoughts and decide what is important, what is realistic, and what needs to be discarded as "trash."

12. Closing. Leave your client with words of encouragement like these:

    - *You can be patient with your thoughts.*

    - *All kinds of thoughts are normal to have.*

    - *You can learn to be friends with the helpful thoughts and walk away from unhelpful thoughts.*

INTERVENTION 30

Thinking About Treatment

This intervention is about helping your client think about the process of treatment for depression. What are his thoughts and beliefs about treatment? Should it help immediately? Should he be better by now? Should life always be good when treatment concludes?

Target skill: Communication. Assessment of thoughts about treatment. Correction of cognitive distortions about treatment and recovery from depression.

1. Check in with your client about his current level of depression and ability to manage his depression using simple scaling questions. Ask him what went well over the past few days. In what ways was he successful in changing his thinking even if difficult things happened? Help your client elaborate on the difference realistic thinking can make.

2. Collaborate with your client on identifying today's task: thinking realistically about treatment. Ask: *What would it be like to apply realistic thinking to the process of treatment? How would realistic thinking about treatment affect him expectations?*

3. Review last week's homework: Was your client able to create a list of thoughts at the end of each day? Take a look at your client's lists together. Marvel at how the brain keeps creating thoughts of all sorts, random, important, beautiful, and distorted. Prompt your client to take a quick look at each thought and label it. Here are some possible labels:

    - Random

    - Important

    - Beautiful

    - Distorted

    - Bothersome

    - Silly

    - Precious

    - Surprising

    Remind your client that he has the power to examine his thoughts. He can put thoughts in their place. He is the captain of his brain!

4. Work with your client on today's task: What are his thoughts about treatment? Begin by collecting your client's thoughts about treatment. Simply have him create a list using the following chart:

Thought about Treatment?	What Kind of Thought?

Figure 83

Then evaluate these thoughts using the same labels ("random," "important," etc.) you used for the thoughts your client listed in his homework (see above).

5. Now help your client explore how his thoughts about treatment may have changed since it started. Here are some examples of how thoughts about treatment can change:

Beginning:	Now:
I should get better within a few weeks.	"Should" kind of thinking often leads me to have depressive thoughts.
I want him (the therapist) to make me better.	I can feel better by thinking better.
I can't even believe that I am here.	I can't even believe that I was smart enough to think about going to treatment. Even though I was in bad shape, I was able to have that good thought.

Figure 84

6. What if your client has gone back to distorted thinking about treatment? This is to be expected, especially in times of stress. This may also be a good way to gauge your client's level of depression. If he has gone back to wanting you to make him better, fast, wonder out loud about his level of depression. Ask about triggers for that kind of thinking. Put the thought in context and

evaluate it together. Be empathic about the thought, but don't assign a faulty label to it.

7. Explore with your client what his thoughts are about ending treatment. Does he have to be depression-free to end treatment? What does "being better" mean to him? Help him create a visual aid for understanding what it means to have made progress:

I know I think better because:	I know I feel better because:	I know I do better because:

Figure 85

Help your client collect evidence about what it means to be better. This is a good way to explore what he has learned in the course of treatment.

8. Summarize today's work with and for your client: You have collected and evaluated thoughts about treatment. You have determined together how his thoughts about treatment have changed. You have also collected evidence about how your client's thoughts, behaviors, and feelings have changed.

9. Assign new homework: Ask your client to write out his thoughts about ending treatment successfully. Then ask him to give each thought a label. Here is a chart he can use:

I am done with treatment if/when . . .	What kind of a thought is this?

I am done with treatment if/when . . .	What kind of a thought is this?

Figure 86

10. Closing. Check in with your client: How does he feel about thinking about being done with treatment? And if he feels scared, is this OK? Is this to be expected? Perhaps it takes some getting used to, and this homework will help him with that!

Interventions Targeting the Emotional Component of the Cognitive Triad

For many of our clients struggling with depression, sadness just seems to come over them and it feels like the feeling is coming out of nowhere. Educating our clients about the cognitive triad can be a tremendous help. Just the understanding that thoughts, feelings, and behaviors are connected might be helpful for them. We are putting their feelings in the proper context. They are not just there. They relate to thoughts and behaviors. Here is how our clients may view depressive feelings without understanding their context:

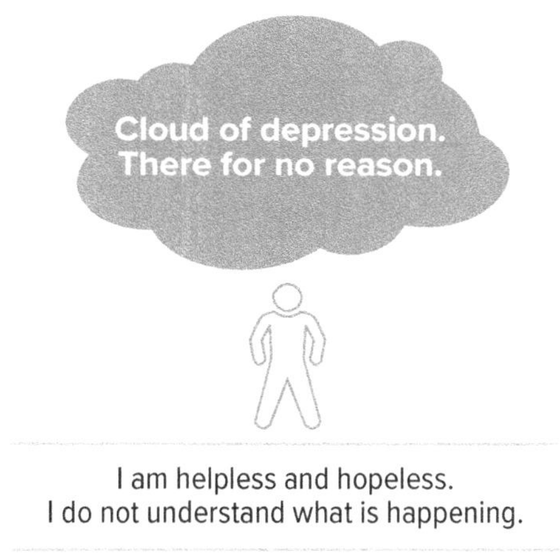

Figure 87

This diagram shows how putting the emotional component of the cognitive triangle in context can help your client gain a better understanding of depression:

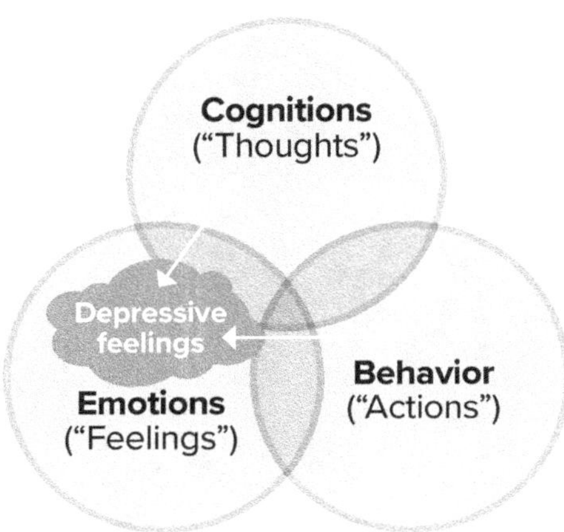

Figure 88

Depressive feelings happen in a context. They do not "fall from the sky." Though there may be a genetic predisposition to depression (and perhaps adverse childhood experiences have amplified this predisposition), depressive feelings can still be impacted by thoughts and behaviors. This means your client does not need to "fall victim" to depression, but can do something about it by thinking and acting differently. This is still true even if the size of the cloud of depression has gotten bigger. The past in not within her control, but the way she thinks about it is. So too are her actions, even if it does not always feel that way.

INTERVENTION 31

Help! My Feelings Are Out of Control

Because your client is likely to have a faulty understanding of what depressive feelings are, it is always a good idea to start with psychoeducation. Out-of-control, intense feelings of depression are often the "doorway" to treatment. No one wants to feel depressed. Most people would like to get rid of their feelings of depression as quickly as possible.

Target skill: Understanding the relationship between thoughts, feelings, and behaviors. Acceptance of feelings. Defusion.

1. Begin with empathy. Welcome your client and ask her what brought her to treatment. Help your client gauge her level of depression using simple scaling questions. In this manner you are beginning to show your client that feelings, just like thoughts and behaviors, can be examined. Listen carefully for overwhelming feelings of hopelessness and helplessness, and suicidal thoughts, feelings, and behaviors. If your client voices those kinds of feelings, dig deeper. Consult with your supervisor about the need to create a safety plan. Don't delay this until the next session. While a safety plan does not guarantee that your client will not hurt herself, it does bring the issue of safety into the room to be examined. Now you both know that feelings of hopelessness and helplessness are present and that you need to do something about this. In very rare cases, if a client cannot or will not consent to a safety plan, a client may need a visit to the ER and an evaluation for hospitalization. Again, consult with your supervisor right away when this appears to be the case.

2. Identify today's task: learning about feelings. Introduce your client to the concept of the cognitive triad using the following image:

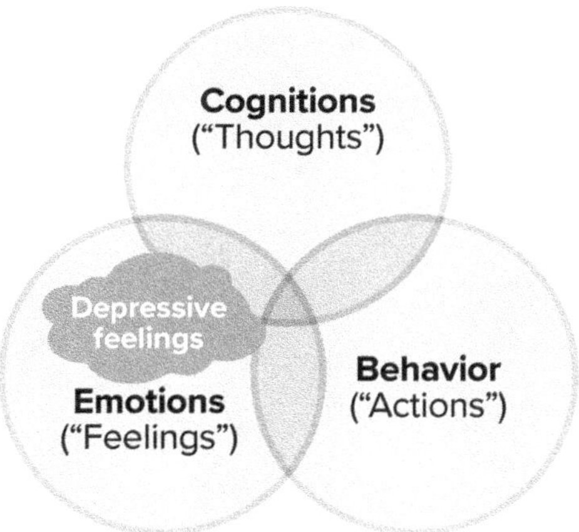

Figure 89

Educate your client about the relationship between feelings, thoughts, and behaviors by adding arrows. To illustrate this, ask your client questions like these:

- *Have you ever felt more depressed after you thought about something?*
- *If you did, what was the something?*
- *Have you ever felt more depressed after you did something?*
- *What was that something?*

You can also reverse this by asking:

- *Have you ever felt less depressed after you thought about something?*
- *If you did, what was the something?*
- *Have you ever felt less depressed after you did something?*
- *What was that something?*

3. Work on today's task: You have now established that feelings are connected to thoughts and behaviors. They do not just "happen" and there are things your client can do to make things better or worse.

4. What if your client talks about using harmful substances to feel better?

    Help your client explore the difference between artificial, short-term feelings of euphoria or numbness and real-world improvement. Real-world improvements can be repeated without harmful side effects. They generally do not cost money and do not require higher doses to sustain effect.

    Say something like this: *I understand that you are in pain, that you just want to get rid of these awful feelings of depression. Let's talk about ways of doing so that are legal and do not cost money.*

    If your client needs integrated treatment for depression and addiction, discuss a plan for integrated treatment with your client and your supervisor.

5. Work with your client on creating an image of her depression using this cloud:

Figure 90

Ask your client to write any depressive feelings that come to mind within the cloud. Or use small clouds, write one feeling on each, and glue or tape them to the larger cloud. Here are a few little clouds to cut out:

Figure 91

With the latter approach, you are also teaching your client that her big cloud of depression is actually made of many different components. Each depressive feeling can be examined by asking: Is this feeling valid? Is it solidly connected with reality as it is right now? Or is this feeling related to something that has long passed? Does this feeling "fit" things as they are right now?

Let your client be creative when working with the clouds. Keep crayons, markers, and colored pencils ready. The more your client illustrates her feelings of depression, the more she can learn about examining those feelings.

6. Summarize with and for your client what you have done together so far: Your client has learned feelings are connected to thoughts and behaviors, and you have illustrated this by using the cognitive triad. You have also helped your client name her feelings of depression using the depression cloud(s). By doing so you have helped your client understand that that big feeling of depression can be made up of feelings about many different things.

7. Assign homework: Send your client home with the image of her depression cloud(s). Ask your client to write something she can think or do to respond realistically to each of those feelings. If she struggles with this, encourage her to ask a family member or friend for assistance.

8. Closing. Check in with your client: Does she understand that there are connections between the way she feels, what she does, and what she thinks? Explain that just because there are connections between feelings, behaviors, and thoughts, this does not mean she is to blame for her depression. Say clearly that she did not cause her depression, but that she can do things to make it better.

9. What if your client complains that this is not fair? You could simply agree. But she can still take action to feel better. Not taking action leaves her stuck with depression, which is even less fair.

INTERVENTION 32

I Have a Feeling

There is such a thing as overvaluing feelings. Many of our clients think that because they have a feeling, this feeling is "true." They may show up in treatment having been told to pay attention to their feelings. And they do, to every depressed feeling, every shadow, every cloud. They may not be able to recognize that a feeling can be fleeting and randomly generated. They may not be able to let go of depressive feelings that have outlived their usefulness or were never useful. The following intervention is designed to help your client recognize that feelings, like thoughts, can be random or important, irrelevant or right on.

Target skill: Evaluating feelings. Acceptance. Defusion.

1. Check in with your client about his feelings of depression. How intense were they in the past few days? Was he feeling depressed about specific things? Or did he have a general feeling like a cloud hanging over him? What went well over the past few days? What made him feel happy?

2. Introduce today's task: examining feelings. Ask your client what it would be like if he could let go of some of his feelings of depression. What would it be like if some feelings of depression were outdated, triggered by things that are no longer relevant?

3. Review last week's homework: Take a look at the image your client has brought back to you. Was he able to add things that make him feel better? Is he was not, was he able to seek suggestions from his family or friends? Explore with your client his understanding of the relationship between feelings, thoughts, and behaviors. If your client struggled with this, ask him Socratic questions about what might help him put feelings of depression in perspective. Here is an example of how you could do so.

4. Perhaps your client is feeling depressed, because he feels he has no one to talk to. Ask him:

   - Who was the last person you talked to? What did you talk about?

   - That last person you talked with, how come you talked to him? What made him talk to you?

   - What kind of value is there in the little conversations such as talking to a cashier at the grocery store?

   - How can he make the little conversations count?

5. Work with your client on today's task: looking at depressive feelings as feelings. You can do so using this chart.

Depressive feeling:	What is this feeling telling me?	Is what the feeling is telling me actually true?

Figure 92

Complete this chart with your client. If he struggles with naming feelings related to depression, you can help him by giving him the following feelings list:

- Anger
- Rage
- Loneliness
- Sadness
- Despair
- Frustration
- Feeling lost
- Feeling disconnected
- Hopelessness
- Helplessness

Ask your client what he needs to add to the list.

6. If your client wonders why anger and rage are on the list, explain that depression can make us withdraw or act out and that it's important to look at emotional outbursts in the context of depression.

7. Summarize what you have done so far: Once you have completed the chart with your client, take a moment to explain what you have done together: You have taken a feeling and extracted from it the message it sends him. Then you have considered that the message may be right and appropriate for the situation, or wrong and unrelated.

8. In other words: You have determined that there is nothing wrong with the presence of a feeling, but that there can be something wrong with what the feeling tells you. If a feeling tells you that you are worthless, there is probably evidence that this is not true.

9. Assign new homework: Ask your client to select one feeling from the list. Put it in the following chart and ask him to generate evidence that the message the feeling is sending him is not accurate and realistic. There is no need to find evidence that the feeling is accurate and realistic—he already feels this way.

Depressive feeling:	What is this feeling telling me?	Evidence against the message the feeling is giving me:	Is what the feeling is telling me actually true?

Figure 93

Give your client examples of evidence, such as:

- Other people tell you that you actually are capable.

- You have actually accomplished something in the past.

- There are moments when you do feel happy.

10. Closing. Check in with your client. Does he understand what it means to look at evidence? If he expresses doubts about finding evidence, ask him to enlist the help of his best friends and family members. Explain that depression may make it difficult to examine feelings and that it is OK to rely on friends and family for help.

INTERVENTION 33

Talking to Your Depression

Once your client understands that a feeling itself can't do much harm but listening to the messages that the feeling sends can, you have opened the door to having a conversation with a feeling. The following intervention is designed to help your client converse with her depressive feelings and to question the messages those feelings are sending her.

Target skill: Questioning the validity of feeling messages. Interacting with depressive feelings. Defusion.

1. Begin with empathy. Check in with your client about her level of depression and ability to manage her feelings of depression. What went well over the past few days? Where did she get stuck? And if she did get stuck, how did she attempt to get unstuck?

2. Introduce today's task: interacting with depressive feelings. You could also call it a debate. In this debate she can question her depressive feelings, reason with them, and even refuse to engage with them if they are particularly unreasonable.

3. Review last week's homework: Was your client able to collect evidence against the message her depressive feeling was giving her? If not, was she able to ask family or friends to assist with this? What did it feel like to "take on" the message that depression sent her? Was this empowering? Frightening? No matter what, your client has begun to realize that it is possible to question the messages that depression sends her.

4. Work on today's task: You are going to role-play with your client. Your client will be the voice of depressive feelings and you will be the voice of reason. Your conversation might go something like this:

   Client: I feel so depressed. This is not worth it. I can't do this anymore. I feel out of options.

   You: Well, hello there, depressive feelings. I knew you would be here today. Still trying to sell that terrible message?

   Client: But things are terrible. There is nothing left to talk about. This is it.

   You: Wait a minute! What are you talking about? Not everything is terrible.

   Client: It is! It's over.

   You: So I am wondering about your dog. Are things terrible with your dog? Does it feel terrible to *feed or cuddle with your dog?*

   Client: Well, no, of course not. The dog is what keeps me going.

   You: So the dog is something, the dog keeps you going in spite of the messages that depression sends you.

   Client: (Reluctant) Well, yes, I guess so, but that's not enough.

You: Wow, another one of those messages. Why is the dog not enough? I bet the dog would disagree.

You get the idea. Just keep questioning the truthfulness of the messages the depressive feelings are sending.

5. Now ask your client to switch roles. You are now taking the role of depression and your client will be the voice of reason. See how it goes.

6. Once you are done with the second role play, ask your client what it was like to take on the voice of reason. Was it difficult? Were there moments of humor? What does it feel like to argue with the messages depression sends?

7. Summarize what you have done together so far: Both you and your client have been the voice of reason and the voice of depression. Your client tried on the role of the voice of reason. Stress that there is always something the voice of reason can say to the messages that depressive feelings send.

8. Assign new homework: Ask your client to interview her friends and family about the voice of reason. Ask her to collect examples of how other people interact with the difficult feelings and the messages they send. Ask your client to record the person's name, the difficult feeling, and how he or she interacts with the messages that feeling sends, using an index card as shown below.

Name:

Difficult Feeling:

How _________________ interacts with the message
the difficult feeling sends:

Figure 94

9. Closing. Leave your client with words of encouragement like these:

   - *Difficult feelings don't have to be scary.*

   - *You can interact with them.*

   - *You can take care of them.*

   - *And in the process of this you can take care of yourself.*

INTERVENTION 34

The Fear of Feeling Depression

This intervention is designed to help your client recognize that feelings of depression, and feelings related to and contained in depression, are not in themselves dangerous. They may be unpleasant. They may feel unbearable. But they are just feelings, a construct of the brain with no more power than we give them. When you remove the power source from feelings, you reduce the power of depression. This intervention is for those clients who are afraid of their depressive feelings and the intensity they can bring with them.

Target skill: Interacting with depressive feelings without fear. Acceptance. Defusion.

1. Begin with empathy. Check in with your client about his current level of depression and ability to manage his feelings. How does he currently experience his depressive feelings? Are they overwhelming? Or just annoying? How tired is he of his depressive feelings?

2. Introduce your client to today's task: getting rid of the fear of depression in order to take away the power of depressive feelings. Ask: *What would it be like if depression was just there, but you were not afraid of it?*

3. Review last week's homework: What did your client find out from family and friends? What kinds of difficult feelings do they experience? Help your client understand that difficult feelings are part of being human. Sometimes they are present, sometimes they are not. But no one is exempt from having difficult feelings. How do his family and friends interact with their difficult feelings? Do they simply dismiss them? Are they afraid of them? If they are, what do they do about their fear? Is there anything useful your client can "poach" to better be able to interact with his feelings of depression?

4. Work on today's task: getting rid of the fear of depression. Compare fear to a battery. Once depressive feelings get "plugged in" to the battery of fear, they have more power. Fear is the power source that keeps depression going and amplifies it. Here is an image you can use to explain:

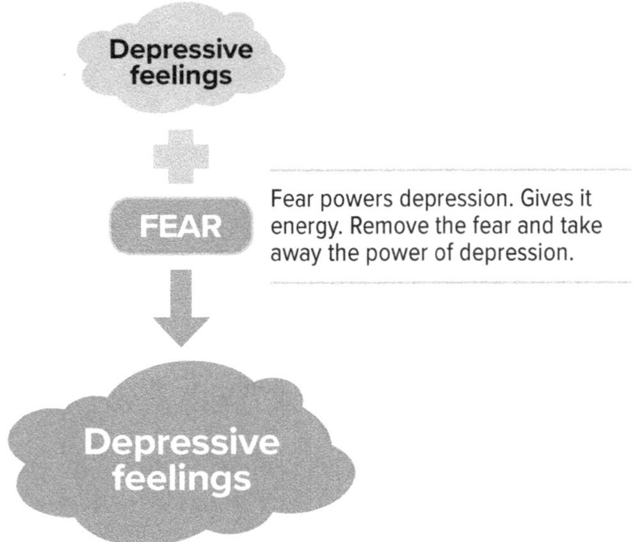

Figure 95

5. How can your client unplug the power source? Go back to exploring the
    many ways in which depression is a con man. Here are some of the lies that
    depression may tell:

    - You should be afraid of me.

    - You should spend all of your time with me.

    - You should spend all of your energy trying to interact with me.

    - I am the most important thing in the world.

    - You are nothing without me.

    - I am who you are.

6. Explain to your client that the key to getting rid of the fear of depressive
    feelings is to unplug from it. That means refusing to believe the many lies
    depression tells him. Depressive feelings can be a bully who always wants
    more.

7. Here are some ways your client may want to interact with his depressive
    feelings without plugging into fear. He may say to his feelings:

    - I am afraid of you, but that does not stop me from walking away from
      you.

    - I choose to spend my time with meaningful things and people.

    - I choose to spend my energy on meaningful things and people.

    - You are there. Sometimes you seem important, but you are definitely
      not the most important thing in the world.

    - I am a (mother/child/aunt/teacher, etc.).

- You are a part of me right now, but you are not me. I am so much more than you can ever imagine.

8. Now role-play an interaction between depressive feelings and helpful responses. First, you will be playing the role of helpful responses. Then switch and your client will respond to the con man of depression in helpful ways.

9. Be creative. You don't have to stick with the script. Elaborate. Put depressive feelings and the fear of them in their place.

10. When you are done, help your client reflect on his experience. What was it like to be the voice of fear? What was it like to be the voice of reason? Which statement made by the voice of reason fits him best? This should be the statement he carries around with him for the next week.

11. Summarize what you have done so far today: You have examined the role of fear in making depression bigger. You have explored the idea of unplugging from fear and role-played ways in which this can be done.

12. Assign new homework: Together with your client, create an index card for him to carry around. Use the most meaningful statement by the voice of reason. Ask your client to decorate the card. It should be pretty so that your client wants to look at it. Here is an example of what an index card could look like:

Figure 96

13. Ask your client to look at this card frequently when he becomes afraid of depressive feelings. In this case, your client may want to do something meaningful or meet up with someone to avoid succumbing to the fear of depression.

14. Closing. Explain again that not giving in to the fear of a feeling can be helpful. It does not mean that the depression goes away, but it may mean that your client does not give it power, does not let it get bigger. Check in with your client about any questions he may have.

INTERVENTION 35

Wearing the Heavy Blanket of Depression

Sometimes clients are not afraid of their depressive feelings. They have had them for so long that they can't imagine life without them. It may feel as if depression is actually a part of them. For this kind of client, letting go of feelings of depression and viewing them as "just" feelings can be difficult. They are, in a sense, at home in their depression. Anything else feels uncomfortable.

This intervention is designed to help these clients think of their depressive feelings as a cloak or coat. The cloak is comfortable most of the time. But it is worn every day even when it is not needed, such as on a hot summer day.

Target skill: Evaluating and letting go of depressive feelings. Creating and accepting change.

1. Begin with empathy. Check in with your client about her current level of depressive feelings and her ability to manage them. Ask what went well over the past few days. What was difficult? In what way did depression impact your client? What did she think, feel, and do that had nothing to do with her depression?

2. Introduce your client to today's task: taking off the heavy cloak of depression by allowing herself to feel other things, even if these feelings are unfamiliar and perhaps uncomfortable. Say something like this:

    > *Feelings of depression have been around for you for such a long time that they just feel like a natural part of your life. In a sense they are comfortable, because they are what you know. But there is another way of being. It is possible to "step out," to take off the heavy blanket of depression. While it feels familiar and protective, it stops you from having new experiences. It's not that you like your depression. You are just used to it.*

3. Review last week's homework with your client: Did she carry her index card? Ask her to describe at least one situation in which she used it. How were her depressive feelings trying to con her? What was it like to respond to them using the index card? Was she able to identify and engage in meaningful action or human contact after she used the card?

4. Work on today's task using the following exercise. You will need a big blanket that allows a little light to come through, such as a knitted blanket. Invite your client to participate in an experiment that involves getting under a blanket. If your client struggles with claustrophobia, this intervention is not for her.

5. To ensure that your client feels safe during this exercise, sit at a slight distance and explain that you will remain seated but that your client will be able to hear your voice. Explain that she will only be under the blanket for about 2 minutes.

6. Ask your client to get completely under the blanket. If her feet stick out, this is OK. Ask your client to notice what it feels like.

7. While she is under the blanket ask her the following kinds of questions:
   - Is this a cozy place to be?
   - Is it warm?
   - Is it comfortable?
   - What can you see?
   - Can you see me?

8. After 1 to 2 minutes, ask your client to remove the blanket. Explain that if she likes the blanket, she can still wrap it around herself for comfort.

9. Help your client explore the answers to the questions. What was comfortable about the experience? What was uncomfortable? How much was she able to see through the blanket?

10. Ask your client to think of depression as a blanket. The cover of depressive feelings feels right. It can be protective. But it also takes away from the experience of life. Through the blanket, your client was not able to fully see what was around her. In the same manner, depressive feelings can keep her from seeing the world clearly.

11. Where is the blanket now? If your client is still wearing it but her head is sticking out, talk about this with your client. It is possible to take off the heavy blanket of depressive feelings one step at a time. If your head sticks out, you can already see more clearly. And if you can see clearly, you can think more clearly.

12. Summarize with and for your client what you have done so far: You have explained that wearing the blanket of depressive feelings can feel protective. You have engaged in an experiment to help your client explore how the blanket of depressive feelings might affect her.

13. Assign new homework: Ask your client to create a list of ways in which her depressive feelings are protective and ways in which they keep her from fully participating in life. You can use the following template:

Ways in which my depressive feelings are protective:	Ways in which they keep me from fully participating in life:

Figure 97

Ask your client to bring this template to your next meeting.

14. Closing: You have established that depressive feelings can seem protective, but that they can also be a barrier to fully participating in life. Explain that it is possible to symbolically "take off the blanket of depression" and enter life one step at a time. If your client feels the urge to get back under the blanket, this is to be expected. She can take off the blanket again when she is ready.

INTERVENTION 36

Peeking Out from Under the Blanket: Feeling Other Feelings

This intervention is designed to help your client "peek out" from under the blanket of depressive feelings and allow herself to recognize and feel some other feelings. The intervention can also be helpful if your client would like to try doing some new things but needs a little push.

Target skill: Recognizing and accepting a range of feelings. Tolerating change. Developing curiosity.

1. Check in with your client about her current level of depression and ability to manage depressive feelings. Are things moving in the right direction? In what way does your client feel stuck? In what way has she become unstuck? What does it feel like to become unstuck?

2. Introduce today's task: feeling some new feelings. You can introduce the idea by using the "peeking out from under the blanket" metaphor. There are all of these new sights and sensations—what happens when they turn into feelings?

3. Review last week's homework: Explore with your client the ways her depressive feelings are protective. What do they protect her from? And in what ways do they keep her from fully participating in life?

4. Work on today's task: feeling some new feelings. You may want to start with a "small" feeling, such as curiosity. Ask your client to participate in an experiment. For this experiment you will need a strange fruit—for example, you can use a seed from a pomegranate.

5. Ask your client to look at the seed. Does she feel a bit curious? Where does she think the seed comes from? What would a fruit containing this seed look like? Ask your client to wonder out loud about the seed? What country might it come from? Does she think she could grow this in her backyard?

6. Help your client recognize the feeling of curiosity if she has it, and if she does not, help her reflect on this. Is her lack of curiosity self- protective? Is it linked to a fear of disappointment? If she is not curious about this seed, are there other things she is curious about?

7. Continue the experiment. Ask your client if she wonders about the taste of the seed. From the way it looks, what should it taste like?

8. Finally, ask your client to taste the seed. Is the taste what she expected? Or is it a complete surprise? How did she feel when tasting the seed?

9. Summarize what you have done together so far: You have introduced the idea that it is OK to try on some other feelings. You have explored the feeling of curiosity. You have asked your client to follow her curiosity and taste the pomegranate seed.

10. Collaborate on developing new homework related to feeling curious: Help your client identify one thing or person she is curious about and a way to

follow through with her curiosity. Ask her to keep a record of her experiences and bring it to the next session. Be sure to explain that it is a good idea to start small.

Here is a template you can use for this assignment:

The thing/person I feel curious about:	Ways in which I can follow the feeling of curiosity and experience the thing I am curious about:

Figure 98

Lastly, ask her to follow through and make a record of her experience on the back of the template. How did she feel during the experience? Does she consider it a success?

11. Closing. Check in with your client. Does she have any questions about the assignment? Was it OK to try something new?

INTERVENTION 37

Getting to Know Depressive Feelings: Sadness

Many of our clients struggle with understanding the range of emotions they experience when depressed. They may also struggle with accepting an emotion. Perhaps they just want it to go away. Or they may embrace one emotion, such as anger, to keep another, like sadness, at bay. The following interventions are designed to educate your client about emotions that are common with depression. They are, in fact, common human emotions, but they can be amplified in depression and may take up a lot of space and time.

Target skill: Feelings exploration, acceptance. Listening to feelings. Defusion.

1. Check in with your client. How is she feeling today? When she names a feeling, ask her to elaborate. If she is feeling sad, can she pinpoint what triggered the feeling? If she is feeling lonely, who would she like with her?

2. Introduce your client to today's task: getting to know sadness. Explain that the purpose of this exercise is not to dwell more on sadness, but to get to know sadness better. Explain that within every feeling, there is a message. Also explain that you are going to continue to look at feelings as feelings as opposed to powerful entities.

3. Review last week's homework: How did the exercise in curiosity go? Take a look at your client's homework sheet with her. Who or what was she curious about? Did she take steps to be more curious and experience something new? If she did, how did it go? If she did not, what stood in the way?

4. Work on today's task: The first thing you are going to do is explore again with your client the nature of feelings. You can use the following image:

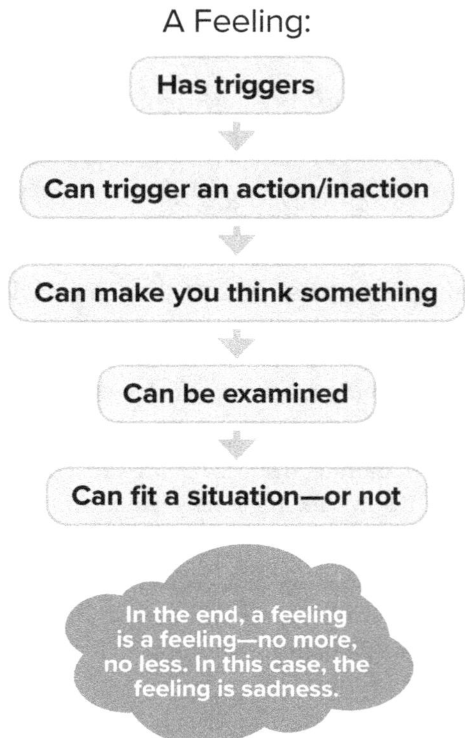

Figure 99

Ask your client to name a sad feeling and walk through this image with her:

- Does she know what triggered her sadness?
- What did she do or not do based on her sadness?
- What did she think based on her sadness?
- Was she able to examine her sadness? If not, she is doing this now!
- Did the sadness fit her situation or was it based in something long gone?

5. You have now established again that sadness is a feeling that can be examined and relates to her thinking and her actions. Your client's sadness does not need to be powerful. She can assign it a place in her life (not too big, not too small). Because she is suffering from depression, it is likely that her sadness is taking up a lot of space in her life. Are there ways to shrink this space? Here are some suggestions:

- Shrink the space sadness is taking up by doing more things that take full attention, such as helping others.
- Give the sadness a designed amount of time and attention, then let it go. If it demands more time and attention, your client can renegotiate

this. Does your client think giving the sadness more time and space will help her? Or is sadness just being a bully that wants all of her time?

6. Role-play the conversation your client needs to have with her feeling of sadness. Your client will be herself, and you will be her sadness. Here is how this may go:

> **Client:** I am feeling OK today. Maybe I will go and see Jen.
>
> **Sadness:** No, no, no. Look outside. It is such a dreary day. Nothing good can come of it. Stay inside. Remember your cat? She suffered so much when she died. And you are suffering, too. Sit. Or sleep. There is so much sadness in the world, how can you go and enjoy yourself? That's just wrong!
>
> **Client:** Oh, my cat. That was so sad, how much she suffered. I miss her so much.

You get the idea where this is going. Sadness demands more sadness. Sadness does not want to let your client go!

7. Now: Ask your client to role-play again. Only this time, she should not give in so easily to sadness. She should use rational arguments to put sadness in its place. Ask your client if she is up for this. Could she come up with responses to sadness? If she cannot, you can give her the following script:

> **Client:** I am feeling OK today. Maybe I will go and see Jen.
>
> **Sadness:** No, no, no. Look outside. This is a terrible day. It reminds you of terrible things like the day your cat died a horrible death.
>
> **Client:** That was a long time ago. I do miss that cat. She was so cuddly. I'm still going outside. I want to connect with Jen. She also loved the cat. We can remember her together.
>
> **Sadness:** You are a bad person. How can you forget about your cat? You should remember her every day. She deserves your sadness. You are being selfish.
>
> **Client:** This is silly. I am not selfish. I am just going to Jen's house. She also remembers my cat. We had such good times together. I am going to think of the good times.
>
> **Sadness:** You. Need. To. Be. Sad! Devastated. Inconsolable. This is the only thing that matters.
>
> **Client:** Enough. I am just going. Sadness, take care of yourself. I will check on you later.

8. Check in with your client. What did it feel like to talk back to sadness? Did it feel like a revolt? Like treason? Or was it OK? Is it, in fact, OK to recognize that sadness is there, but then walk away from it to engage in life?

9. Summarize what you have done so far: You have explored the nature of feelings. You have reiterated that a feeling is just a feeling, even sadness. You have role-played how to put sadness in its place when it becomes too pushy. And you have explored what it feels like when you do.

10. Assign new homework: Ask your client to create a place and time to recognize sadness in her daily schedule. Explain that at other times, when sadness is demanding that she spend all of her time with it, your client should go on with her life and do the things she was planning to do.

11. Once your client has identified a time and a place to recognize sadness, ask her to do the following:

    - Welcome the sadness.

    - Ask her sadness what it wants.

    - Respond to her sadness with kindness.

    - Let go of her sadness, agreeing to "see" her again at the designated place and time the following day.

12. Closing. Check in with your client and make sure she understands the instructions. You may want to give your client an index card containing instructions for welcoming sadness and letting it go.

INTERVENTION 38

Getting to Know Depressive Feelings: Anger

For some who struggle with depression, it is easier to be angry than to be sad. For them anger is an expression of sadness. It may be difficult to face sadness. It may be easier to be angry—with the world, oneself, or others. In this case, it will be useful for your client to recognize anger as an expression of sadness. Additionally, those who are around or live with your client (or even your client herself) may benefit if she is able to recognize anger as sadness.

Target skill: Feelings exploration, acceptance. Listening to feelings. Defusion.

1. Begin with empathy. Ask your client about different kinds of feelings she has experienced over the past week. Ask her to elaborate. What made her feel sad, frustrated, happy, silly? Was it OK to have all of those feelings?

2. Introduce your client to today's task: getting to know anger as an expression of sadness. Ask your client if she can relate to this. Does her sadness ever "flip" to anger?

3. Review last week's homework: Was your client able to find a time and place to recognize her sadness every day? What did her sadness say to her? Was she able to respond to her sadness with kindness?

   Was she able to let her sadness go at the end of the designated time period? If she was not, perhaps it felt "artificial" to let go of the sadness during the exercise. Explain that this is OK. It takes practice to give a feeling a time and a place and then move on.

4. If your client expresses that it feels like she is denying her sadness, explain that you are looking for her to do the opposite: Give the feeling of sadness a time and a place. Letting it be a feeling, no less and no more.

5. Introduce today's task: getting to know anger as an expression of sadness. To help your client understand the idea, take out a coin. Show your client that it has two sides. Explain that sadness is similar to this, that often the other side of sadness is anger (or something like anger). Explain that often, but not always, anger is an expression of sadness. Here is an example to illustrate the point:

   > Kason's father recently died in a motorcycle accident. Kason cries himself to sleep every night. He does not want to think or talk about his father's death to his mother or anyone else. When his mother tries to help by asking his uncle to talk to him, Kason screams: "I hate you. I hate him. I hate all of this. Leave me alone."

6. Ask your client to elaborate on what might really be going on here. Is Kason feeling angry? It does seem like he is. But is he feeling anything else?

7. Now ask your client to think about herself. Does she ever feel a wave of anger washing over her when she is actually sad?

Be sure to normalize anger as an expression of sadness. Say something like this:

> *We all do this. It can be so difficult to feel sadness, because it can make us feel vulnerable. Anger, however, makes us feel more powerful. When we are angry, it seems like we have at least some power.*

8. Listen with kindness as your client explores how she sometimes turns sadness into anger. Don't demonize anger.

9. When your client is done talking about her anger, ask her what she thinks is behind it. If it is sadness, can she make room for it, recognize it, listen to it with kindness, and then let it go? (See the prior intervention.)

10. Another way to approach this is to think of anger as a mask. Anger often, but not always, masks sadness. Of course, there are situations in which we are legitimately angry.

11. Summarize what you have done so far: You have introduced the idea that anger can be an expression of sadness, the other side of the coin. You have examined how this can be the case for others and also for your client. You have normalized the experience. You have asked your client to think what may be behind her feelings of anger. What is she sad about? You have asked your client to recognize her sadness and make room for it.

12. Assign new homework: Give your client a piece of paper with the drawing of a coin. Write *anger* on one side and *sadness* on the other side. Be sure to make the drawing big so your client can add to it. Here is a template for a coin:

Cut out the coin shapes and glue
them together, letters facing outward.

Figure 100

13. From the way the coin looks, it is obvious that anger is often louder than sadness. Ask your client to write a note on the coin when she gets angry, stating who she is angry with and why.

14. Ask her to then turn the coin over and write on the sadness side what might be behind her anger. What is it that she needs or wants? Is she sad because she is missing something or someone?

15. Ask your client to bring the coin to your next meeting. Check in with your client before she leaves. Does she understand the assignment?

16. If your client is a child, it may be enough to simply ask her to carry the coin with her and talk with her family about sadness and anger and how they connect.

17. Closing. Leave your client with words of encouragement like these:

    - *Think of anger as an expression of sadness.*

    - *Then be kind to the sadness and to yourself.*

INTERVENTION 39

Getting to Know Depressive Feelings: Despair—A Call to Action

Sadness is one thing—despair is another. Despair is the "no way out" feeling. Despair weighs heavily on the person who feels it and makes it difficult to take any action. This intervention is designed to help your client recognize that despair is always a call to action precisely because despair tells you that nothing can be done.

Target skill: Feelings exploration, acceptance. Listening to feelings. Defusion. Connecting feelings with meaningful action.

1. Begin with empathy. Check in with your client about her current level of depression and her ability to manage her depression. Are things moving in the right direction? Is your client beginning to realize how feelings relate to her overall level of depression? Are there feelings she tries to avoid? If so, why? Has she begun to welcome some difficult feelings?

2. Introduce today's task: recognizing the feeling of despair as a call to action. Say something like this:

    Despair tells you that there is no way out and nothing can be done to change the situation. But this is one of the lies that depression tells you. Despair is actually a big red blinking light: It makes you aware that things have to change.

3. Review last week's homework: Take a look at the "flip side" coin. Was your client able to connect anger with sadness? Was she able to look beyond her anger and recognize what need or want it was expressing? Validate your client's needs as appropriate and help her identify ways of getting them met without resorting to anger.

4. Work on today's task: recognizing despair and using it as a way to make important changes.

5. Begin by collecting all the thoughts that lead to feelings of despair. Ask your client to give examples and write them on a piece of paper. Here are some sample thoughts of despair:

    - I will be stuck here forever.

    - I will feel like this forever.

    - There is no help.

    - There is no hope.

    - I have no one.

    - No one understands me and no one will ever be able to.

6. Remind your client that just as feelings are just feelings, thoughts are just thoughts. They may not accurately represent what is truly going on. Never-

theless, if your client's feelings are impacted by the thoughts of despair listed above, what does this really mean?

7. Help your client translate thoughts of despair into calls to action. In other words: If she does not want to feel despair (and who does?), she can take action, one step at a time. Help her make a wants/needs list like this:

   - I want to move on. I want to get out of here

   - I don't want to feel like this anymore.

   - I want and need help.

   - I want to feel hopeful.

   - I want and need the company of others.

8. Help your client recognize the bigger picture: that she wants a meaningful and connected life, the opposite of feeling despair every day.

9. Ask your client how she could move from feeling despair to living a meaningful and connected life. Collect her ideas.

10. If she struggles with this, ask her to pretend that she already is living a meaningful and connected life and to describe it to you. Note all of the components of this life that she talks about.

11. Take out a poster board and create a plan like this:

Parts of my meaningful and connected life:	Everyday steps I can take to get there:

Figure 101

Make the plan pretty! You can add images using art materials, photos, and even pages from magazines.

12. When you get to the "step" part, ask your client to be concrete. The steps should be everyday steps, things she can actually do. Here is an example:

    Perhaps your client's despair is rooted in her loneliness. She wants to have meaningful relationships, but she is not ready to join a class or a group. She could start by volunteering at an animal shelter. This would introduce her again to feeling connectedness.

13. Summarize with and for your client what you have done so far: You have recognized the feeling of despair as a trickster: Despair tells you that nothing can be done, but in fact signals that action is needed. You have identified unmet needs and wants on which despair is based and have envisioned a meaningful and connected life. You have also identified steps your client can take toward a meaningful life. It may be helpful to use this image to illustrate what you have done so far.

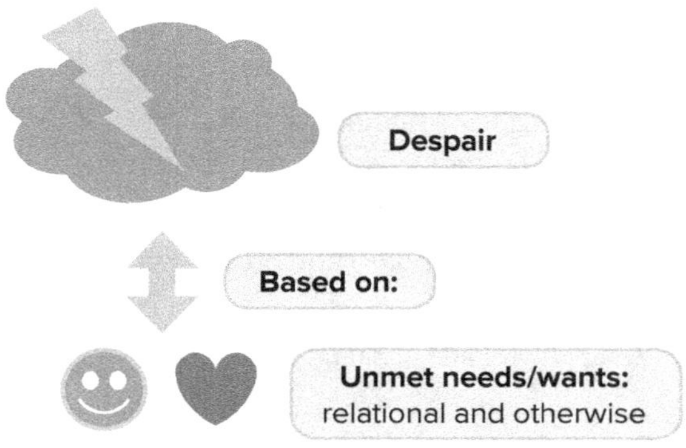

Figure 102

14. Your client may ask if she will stop feeling despair tomorrow. You can use the following illustration to help her understand that walking away from despair is a step-by-step process, not a giant leap:

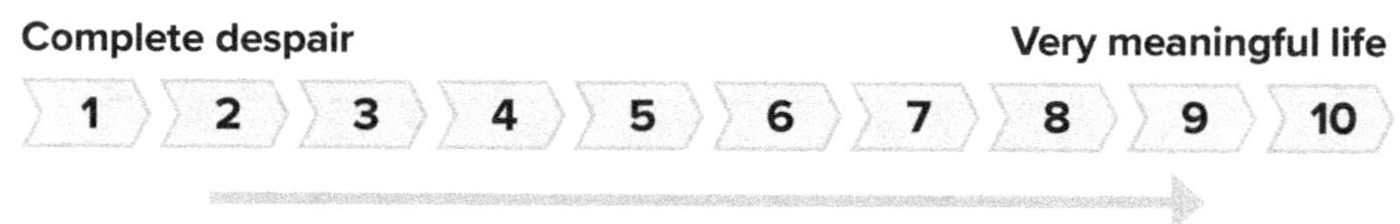

Figure 103

Explain that every step away from despair is a step toward a meaningful and connected life, no matter how small the step is. Also help your client understand that almost no one lives a life in which every minute is meaningful—that would be an unrealistic expectation.

15. Assign new homework: Ask your client to select one step from her list and take this step daily over the next few days. Be sure that it is a workable step such as:

    - Make human connections in person or by phone
    - Step out of the house
    - Draw
    - Write
    - Sing
    - Dance

16. Ask your client to keep a record of the steps she has taken on a note card and record how she felt right after. Be sure to check in with your client about any questions. It may be best to ask your client to write her step and the time of day at which she will take it on an index card. She can then check off her step every day and bring the card to your next session.

17. Closing. Leave your client with words of encouragement like these:

    - *Despair can be a meaningful signal to make changes.*
    - *You can take steps toward a meaningful like.*
    - *Every step counts.*
    - *You matter.*

INTERVENTION 40

How to Make It Happen: Feeling Present Right Here, Right Now

This intervention is designed for clients who are often not quite with you. They are sitting in front of you but seem engaged with thoughts and feelings related to the past. How can they be fully present in a way that is pleasant but not artificial?

Target skill: Mindful presence. Acceptance.

What you will need: A small item to taste such as a raisin, M&M, or hard candy. Be sure to have a sugar-free item for your diabetic clients.

1. Begin with empathy. Check in with your client about his current level of depression and ability to manage his depression. Does he feel his life is moving in the right direction? Can he attend to all kinds of feelings, difficult and pleasant?

2. Introduce today's task: learning to be present right here, right now, using mindful attention. Explain that many of us are either stuck in the past or worried about the future. The challenge is to "be here now," especially for your client who is struggling with depressive feelings.

3. Review last week's homework: Take a look at the index card your client brought. Was your client able to take everyday steps toward a meaningful life? What steps did he take? How did he feel when he took them? You can take out last week's arrow depicting small steps to a meaningful life and ask him to mark where he sees herself now.

4. Work on today's task: Ask your client to participate in an experiment. You will need a single raisin or other small food item, such as an M&M or Skittle. Explain that the experiment involves eating the item.

5. Explain to your client that he will put the raisin in his mouth, but not bite into it. He should let the raisin rest on his tongue with his mouth closed until he can no longer resist the urge to bite into it. He should then pay attention to the taste.

6. Give your client the raisin and ask him to go ahead with the experiment. It may be best if you participate too.

7. When you are both done with the experiment, ask your client what he was thinking about during the experiment. Was it easy to wait to bite into the raisin? Did his mouth water? Did he try to delay biting into the raisin? When he did bite into the raisin, what did he taste?

8. Listen to all of the answers your client gives. Then say this something like this:

   When you had the raisin in your mouth you were truly present in the moment. Your senses were responding to the raisin. Your mouth was watering. Your brain was sending signals to get you to bite into the raisin. You were right there. You were not in the past. You were not worried about the future. You were present with the raisin.

9. Ask if the raisin experiment reminds your client of any other experiences that make him feel present in the moment. Explain that being fully present can often be connected with the senses:

    - Touch

    - Taste

    - Smell

    - Hearing

    - Sight

10. Ask your client which one of these senses makes him feel most present.

11. Summarize what you have done so far: You have engaged in an experiment to help your client be present in the moment. You have learned that being fully present is often connected with a strong sensory experience, and your client has explored which sense he best relates to.

12. Assign new homework: Ask your client to repeat the raisin experiment every day at a designated time, perhaps at the end of the day, but at least an hour before bed. It could mark the transition from work to leisure.

13. Closing. Check in with your client. Does he have any objections to using the raisin experiment? If he does, how can he alter the experiment to make it work for him?

INTERVENTION 41

Expanded Presence—Right Here, Right Now

The last intervention focused on helping your client to be present, using the senses to expand positive feelings. The following intervention is designed to expand this experience. No materials are needed—not even a raisin!

Target skill: Mindful presence. Openness. Acceptance.

1. Begin with empathy. Help your client gauge her level of depression and ability to manage depression. Are things moving in the right direction? What is your client's relationship with her feelings now? Do they still come over her, seemingly out of nowhere? Or is she able to take a step back, examine her feelings, and embrace those that move her in the direction of a meaningful and connected life?

2. Introduce today's task: expanding mindful presence and focus from a small thing to the entire situation.

3. Review last week's homework: Was your client able to set aside time daily to repeat the raisin experiment? What kinds of feelings did she experience during the experiment? Did she feel silly? Or did she look forward to setting aside time to experience the taste explosion in her mouth? Did the experiment help her feel more present or did it feel like a chore? If your client felt that the experiment was silly, or it felt like a chore, remind her that depression may be sending those faulty messages. Because there is enjoyment involved, depression may be telling her that the experiment is silly because depression does not want her to experience enjoyment. If the experiment felt silly to her, ask her to embrace a "fake it 'til you make it" attitude. She should continue the experiment until it becomes real to her and she enjoys the raisin.

4. Work on today's task: Explain to your client that you will use the room you are currently in to help her become present here and now. Ask her to pick one thing in the room that she likes. It could be anything:

   - The chair she sits in
   - A plant
   - A book
   - The warmth of the room
   - A pillow
   - A picture on the wall

5. Ask your client to take a deep breath and focus her eyes, her thoughts, and her feelings on that item. Explain that her thoughts will wander, and when they do, she can simply bring her attention back to the item. Ask her to embrace its presence. Here is a script:

   Hello there, pillow. You are an old friend. I can always rely on you. So cozy. So soft. You support me, and I really appreciate your presence.

Now: Move on to another item. The item should be bigger in some way. Create a short welcoming meditation for that item. Perhaps you are now moving on to the chair your client is sitting on. Here is what you could say:

Hello there, chair. You are on old friend. You conform to me and make me comfortable. You support me, and I really appreciate your presence.

Use about five to eight items in the room, from small to large, until you've embraced the entire room.

Talking to a pillow or a chair can seem silly or funny. It is OK to laugh. Nevertheless, the pillow is there for your client. You will probably end with a script like this:

Hello there, room. You are an old friend. You are always there for me. You contain the pillow and the chair. You contain me. You give me space for sharing thoughts and feelings. You never judge me. I need you, and I really appreciate your being there for me.

6. When you are done with the exercise, ask your client to once again take a deep breath. Ask what it was like to be fully present in this room and welcome all the components of the room that support her. Did it feel silly? Did she feel gratitude?

7. Explain that feeling present can be a great way to shift attention away from depressive thoughts and feelings. Depressive thoughts and feelings will continue to appear during the exercise. Your client can recognize them, and then move on to presence in the room.

8. Summarize what you have done so far today: You have experienced a way to become fully present by moving your focus from a small item to the entire room. You have recognized how much the things around us support us.

9. Assign new homework: Ask your client to pick a room in her apartment or house where she can repeat the experiment. If your client cannot repeat the experiment at home, ask her to pick another space, perhaps a bench at the playground or a couch in the library. The space does not have to be perfect. Ask your client to repeat the experiment in this space once during the following week. Your client should pick a time and a space now and write it on an index card to remind her of her homework.

10. What if your client feels that she can't come up with things to say to the items she chooses? Write things out for her. Tell her it's OK not to know what to say, it takes time to learn how to talk to a pillow or a chair!

11. Closing. Ask your client if she has any questions. Before she leaves, ask her to be fully present once more in this room. Prompt her to look around and take in all that supports her.

INTERVENTION 42

Expanded Presence—My Corner of the Universe

Your client has learned to expand his attention, moving from a small item to an entire room and looking at the ways in which the space and objects in it support him. The following intervention helps your client expand his attentional focus even more, from the small space he occupies to the large expanse of the universe and back. The key is to help him feel part of the fabric of things big and small and to experience belonging.

Target skill: Mindful presence. Connection with the world and others. Viewing the world as an ally/home.

1. Begin with empathy. Ask how your client is feeling today. Listen and express that you truly appreciate what your client is sharing with you.

2. Introduce today's task: finding a place in this big world, both the small space your client is occupying right now and the wide expanse of the universe. Explain that you are looking to create and feel the experience of belonging.

3. Review last week's homework: Did your client pick a place/thing and expand his attention from the small thing (starting point) to the larger thing (perhaps a room)? Was he able to welcome each part of the space and appreciate how it supports him? What did it feel like to create a connection with the space he occupied? What did it feel like to think of all of these things supporting him?

4. Work on today's task: creating and feeling the experience of belonging and being a part of this wide world. Explain that you will begin, once again, where you are now, focusing on a small item and then moving on from item to item until you get to the larger things that support him, such as the ground under his feet, carrying him and producing food to sustain him. Explain that your client can keep his eyes open or closed, whatever is comfortable. The following script may need to be adjusted to meet your client's needs:

   Take a look around. You are here in this room. Pick an item that supports you in ways you may take for granted.

   There it is:

   This pillow supports you. You feel it behind your back or underneath. It makes things better, more comfortable for you.

   Now, look around again. You and the pillow rest on the chair. You feel the chair behind your back and underneath you. It makes things more comfortable for you. It supports you.

   Now, look around again. You are here in this room. This room shelters you. You are protected from the elements. You can seek comfort in this room. It is your space. This space supports you.

Think of this building. It, too, supports you. It has what you need. A place to eat, a place to sleep, a place to think.

Now, think about the world outside. It, too, supports you. It has what you need. You can go to the store and there will be food. You can go places that interest you. You can see things of great beauty. The world outside feeds your body and your mind.

Think of the ground underneath you. Think of the strange miracle of growing food. Miraculously, the ground produces what we need to live.

No matter what, the ground supports you. It carries you, literally.

Think of the air all around you. You need it to live and it is there, every day.

Think of the earth. It is your home. It supports you. It feeds you. It carries you.

Here you are: with this pillow, on this chair, in this room. A part of the great big world that supports you.

You are at home.

5. When you are done with the script, ask your client to take a deep breath and look around. Ask:

   - Was he able to create the experience of feeling a part of things?

   - If he did, what does it feel like to think of all that is around him as supporting him?

   - Did his mind wander? If it did, this is OK. It is natural.

   - Did your client struggle with feeling connected and supported? If he did, what could make the feelings of connection stronger? In what way does the script of the narrative need to be changed?

6. Summarize with and for your client what you have done so far: You have thought of things big and small that support him, from a pillow to the ground underneath his feet to the air he breathes. You have created a feeling of connection with all that supports him. You have reflected on the connection and on your client's struggles with creating and feeling connection.

7. Assign homework:

   - Print the script for your client and send it home with him.

   - Ask him to change the script in ways that will make it better fit him. He can cross things out, add things, whatever works for him. There is only one rule: Whatever he adds needs to focus on increasing a feeling of belonging and support.

   - Ask your client to read the script to herself every morning or evening at a specific time. Every day he can make changes to it, if he wants.

   - If your client is partnered and he feels comfortable with this, he can also ask his partner to read the script to him.

   - Remind your client that he can impact the way he feels by what he is thinking about and that this homework is one way to do so.

8. Closing. Check in with your client. Does he understand the homework? Are there any barriers to completing the homework? If your client feels that he can only relate to parts of the script, this is OK. He can omit parts he cannot relate to right now.

INTERVENTION 43

Moving into Expression—Feelings on Paper (1)

This intervention adds an element that may take some getting used to for your client. You are going to ask your client to put her feelings on paper using whatever material she is comfortable with. Have a poster board and all kinds of art materials ready.

Target skill: Expression of feelings. Joy and pride in expression of feelings. Communication.

What you will need: Poster board and art materials.

1. Begin with empathy. Check in with your client about her level of depression and her ability to manage depression. Ask:

    In what way have you begun to treat your feelings differently? In what way do you welcome feelings? When you have "out of control" feelings, what do you do with them? Are you beginning to feel and understand that you are in charge of your feelings?

2. Identify today's task: Putting feelings of connection and belonging on paper. Explain that artistic expression is different from using words for feelings. When we make art, we create something that evokes a feeling. If your client has objections to using art to put feelings on paper, ask questions like these:

    - *Are you worried about the images you create?*

    - *Are you worried your artwork will not be good enough or not pretty enough?*

3. Explain that art is not about perfection, but rather about expression. If your client does not want to draw, she can create a collage. Also explain that there are few rules when making art. Color can express feelings by itself. She does not have to draw people and things.

4. Review last week's homework: Did your client make time to read the script every day? Did she make changes to the script? If she did, take a look at the changes together. In what way do they better represent your client's world and increase her feelings of connectedness? How did your client feel when she read the script? Did someone else read the script to her? If so, how does this feel differently?

    Explore the big picture together: Is your client able to evoke feelings of support and connectedness? Can she manage her feelings of depression by creating feelings of connection and comfort?

5. Work on today's task:

    - Provide art materials and a poster board.

    - Because you don't want your client to feel that you are constantly watching her, you too should engage in making art, but not in the same way—you don't want your client to feel that she is competing with you. You could color a printed page or doodle and then color what you doodled.

- Encourage your client to begin by doing something messy. Seeing an empty page can be daunting. She could spill some water on the page to start!

- Invite your client to envision one thing from her script focusing on connection and begin there. She can create an image of herself (stick figure?) next to that thing. She can connect other things that support her. She can use color to represent herself and connect other colors to it. Any visual expression of connection is OK.

- Give your client time. It takes time to get started and a little more time to begin to feel free about making art. While your client is beginning to fill the paper, you should engage in your art activity. If your client has questions, answer them. Conversation about expressing feelings is a good thing. If your client expressed anxiety about putting feelings on paper, compliment her on recognizing her feelings and ask her what she wants to do with those feelings of anxiety. Her anxiety might be sending her a message that is just not true, such as: "You can't do this. It will look awful."

- When your client is done with putting her feelings on paper, compliment her on engaging in the work and praise the work that she has created. Ask her questions like these:

  - *What did it feel like to create artwork?*

  - *Were you afraid to do this?*

  - *Do you think your work has beauty and/or truth in it?*

  - *Were you able to express the feeling of connection?*

6. Summarize what you have done so far: You have introduced your client to the idea of using art to express feelings of connection. Your client has created a work of art and you have explored feelings and meanings related to it.

7. Explain to your client that art is another way to step back and explore and express feelings.

8. Ask your client how she would feel about hanging her artwork on the wall. If she is reluctant, because she feels that it may not be good enough, ask her where she thinks that message may come from and if it is actually true.

9. Assign new homework: Ask your client to take her artwork home and either

   - hang it on the wall and look at it once a day or

   - put it away and look at it once a day.

Explain that your client can add anything she wants to the artwork. There is only one rule: She should not destroy it.

Ask your client to explore her artwork and look for feelings of connection. She should play close attention and make a note of all of her feelings passing through her as she looks at her work.

10. Closing. Check in with your client. Make sure she has a way of getting the poster board home. Have tape handy so she can roll up the work and carry it. Ask your client to bring her work back to your next meeting.

INTERVENTION 44

Moving into Expression: Feelings on Paper (2)

This intervention can build on the previous one or it can stand on its own. It is also about recognizing, creating, and feeling connection using art. It is designed to help your client step in the direction of a meaningful life filled with connections he creates and also feels.

Target skill: Expression of feelings. Recognizing and expression connection. Communication.

What you will need: Poster board and a pen or pencil.

1. Begin with empathy. Help your client gauge his ability to step back from or immerse himself in feelings as needed. Ask him for examples of stepping back from feelings, perhaps because they were not rooted in reality, and immersing himself in another feeling, perhaps because he needs a counterbalance to feelings of depression. Note that, as always, CBT does not ask your client to think only positive thoughts or feel only positive emotions, but rather to think realistic thoughts and feel emotions that correspond to those thoughts.

2. Identify today's task: putting feelings of connection and belonging on paper. In this case, you will be using creative writing. Explain that artistic expression is different from using words for feelings. If your client has objections to using words to put feelings on paper ask:

   - *Are you worried about the words you write?*

   - *Are you worried your words will not be good enough or not pretty enough?*

3. Review last week's homework: Ask your client to take out last week's artwork. Check with him to see if he made any changes to it. If he did, what do those changes mean to him? Look together. Can you find new connections in the work? Ask your client how this work has connected him with his feelings and how it has enabled him to step back and observe his feelings.

4. Work on today's task: Provide a poster board and a pen or pencil.

   - Because you don't want your client to feel that you are constantly watching him, you too should engage in making art, but not in the same way—you don't want your client to feel that he is competing with you. You could color a printed page or doodle and then color what you doodled.

   - Encourage your client to begin by doing something messy. Seeing an empty page can be daunting. He could spill some water on the page to start!

   - Invite your client to envision one thing from his script focusing on connection and to begin writing based on that. Perhaps he wants to write about the pillow supporting him and then about his need to feel more supported. That could lead to writing about people who have supported him. And so forth. Explain again that creative writing does not require logic. He can simply write.

- Give your client time. It takes time to get started and a little more time to begin to feel free about making art. While your client is beginning to fill the paper, you should engage in your art activity. If your client has questions, answer them. Conversation about expressing feelings is a good thing. If your client expressed anxiety about putting feelings on paper, compliment him on recognizing his feelings and ask him what he wants to do with those feelings of anxiety. His anxiety might be sending him a message that is just not true, such as: "You can't do this. It will be awful."

- When your client is done with putting his feelings on paper, compliment him on engaging in the work and on the work that he has created. Ask him questions like these:

  - *What did it feel like to create artwork?*

  - *Were you afraid to do this?*

  - *Do you think your work has beauty and/or truth in it?*

  - *Were you able to express the feeling of connection?*

5. Ask your client if he is willing to read what he has written to you. If he is, listen and then compliment him on his ability to process feelings using creative writing.

6. Once your client has read to you, ask if he is willing to have you read his writing to him. If he is, ask him to just listen.

7. When you are done reading, thank your client for the opportunity to read his work. Ask him what it was like to hear his words spoken by someone else.

8. Summarize what you have done so far: You have introduced your client to the idea of using art to express feelings of connection. Your client has created a work of art and you have explored feelings and meanings related to it. Your client has read his work to you and you have read his work to him. Your client has had an opportunity to "feel" his work when reading it and hearing it.

9. Assign new homework: Ask your client to take his artwork home and designate a time to read it every day. Ask him to observe how his feelings about the work may change over the next few days. Explain that he can add to the work if he wants to. He can also cross things out, but he should not destroy the work. Ask your client to bring his work back to your next meeting.

10. Closing. Ask your client for feedback: Is he becoming more comfortable with expressing and observing his feelings? When can this still be a struggle? Reassure your client that struggles with feelings are a normal part of life.

INTERVENTION 45

Transforming Feelings: Moving into Self-Compassion

Depression, by definition, hurts. It is a whole-person kind of hurt. Often the body hurts in all kinds of ways. Hurtful thoughts and feelings permeate every minute. The spirit feels an incredible amount of exhaustion, the kind that may seem to make it impossible to move. Under these conditions it is difficult not to run with thoughts and feelings that perpetuate depression, such as self -pity, the "why me?" and "why this?" questions that mostly lead nowhere.

This intervention is designed to help your client move into self-compassion. Self-compassion recognizes the suffering, acknowledges the reality of it, and helps the suffering person embrace her whole being. The act of moving from pity and hurt into self-compassion, in spite of the hurt, is a seismic shift, one that moves in the direction of healing.

Target skill: Self-compassion. Valuing feelings.

What you will need: Large cut-out heart and pen or markers.

1. Begin with empathy. Check in with your client regarding her ability to be kind to herself and others in spite of her depressive feelings. Is it easier to be kind to others? Why does she think this is so? Does she consider herself less deserving than others? And if she does, is it possible that this feeling is just a part of depression?

2. Identify today's task: moving into self-compassion. Ask your client what she thinks this might be. Ask about your client's experiences of compassion toward her by others. Has she experienced this and if she did, was she able to accept it?

3. Review last week's homework: Take a look at your client's feelings on paper together. Ask your client to read her work to you again, then read it to her. Has she made changes to it? If she did, what are the changes and what prompted them? But even without changes, how have her feelings about her work changed? Asking the latter question once again reinforces that feelings (even depressive ones) change over time.

4. Work on today's task:

   - Provide your client with a big, cut-out heart and a pen or markers.

   - Ask her to tell you about the most loving and compassionate person in her life. If your client struggles with identifying that person, take time to search. There is almost always someone who is (or was) loving and compassionate, even if that person is no longer in your client's life. Additionally, you can ask about a loving and compassionate higher power or spiritual connection.

   - Ask your client to write into the heart what makes this person so amazing, compassionate, and loving.

Figure 104

- If your client is a child, just change the language. What do you love about _______? What makes her so great? How do you feel when you are with her?

- You can also provide scissors, old magazines, and glue to illustrate what this person is like. Or your client can draw.

- When your client has completed her work, explore it with her. Learn as much as you can about this person by asking Socratic questions, such as: "How do (did) you know that this person is loving? What does this look like in action?"

- Now give your client a second heart cutout. Ask her to apply everything compassionate and wonderful that person has ever said to her to herself, even if she does not believe it yet. Essentially, you are moving words and actions of compassion from one heart to another. Here is an example of what this may look like:

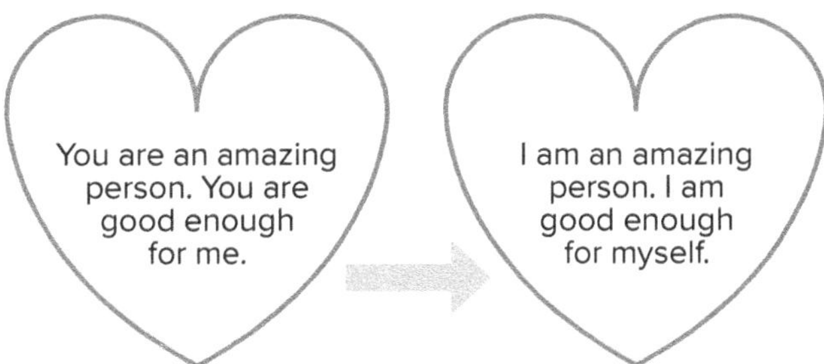

Figure 105

- Move things over one by one. Help your client observe what it feels like to say loving and compassionate things to herself. Can she listen to herself? Is it difficult to say those things? If it is difficult, does she feel that this is because what she is saying to herself is not true? And if she does feel that way, is it possible that this feeling is just part of the range of depressive feelings—in other words, that it is not reflective of the truth?

- Even if it is difficult, try to find at least one compassionate thing your client can now say to herself (perhaps with difficulty, but that is OK).

- If there is more than one thing, this is good, too.

- Use index cards and art materials to create compassion cards for your client to carry around with her. Here is an example of what a compassion card may look like:

Figure 106

5. Assign homework: Ask your client to read the card(s) out aloud at the beginning and end of each day. If she expresses that this may be difficult, ask her to envision the loving and compassionate person she remembers sitting with her as she reads.

6. Closing. Explain that moving into self-compassion takes time and practice. Encourage your client to keep at it, even when this is difficult. Ask if she has any questions about what it means to be compassionate to oneself. If necessary, explain that being compassionate to oneself does not mean lying. It just means to take in the compassion she deserves for who she is: a courageous human being moving in the direction of healing from depression.

Appendix: Selected Figures

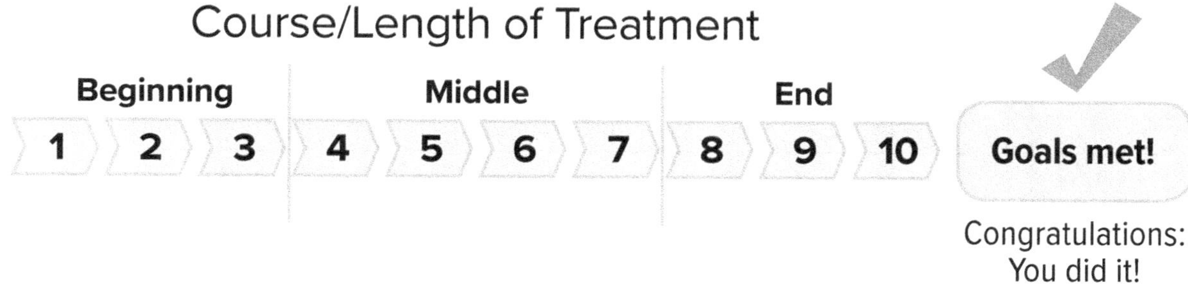

Figure 12

CBT Session Structure
Check-In
Identify Today's Task
Homework Review
Work on Today's Task
Summarize the Work
Identify New Homework
Closing

	Mon	Tue	Wed	Thu	Fri	Sat	Sun
Hours in bed							
Hours of TV							

Figure 13

	Mon	Tue	Wed	Thu	Fri	Sat	Sun
Contacted friend/family member X							

Figure 14

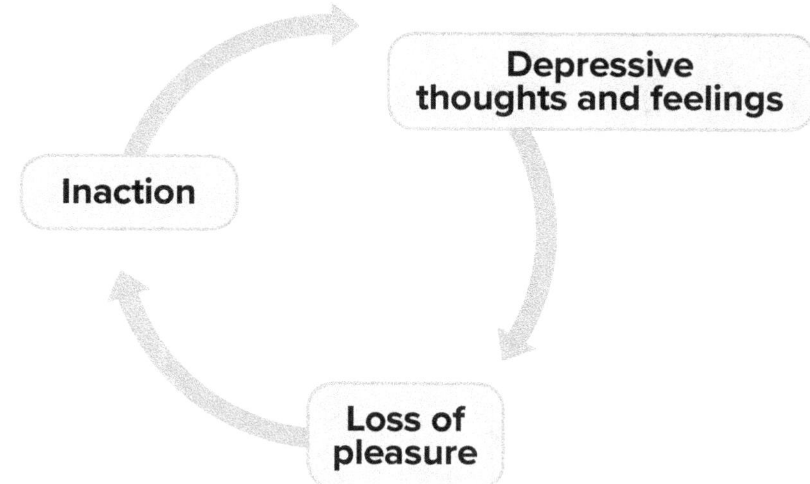

Figure 15

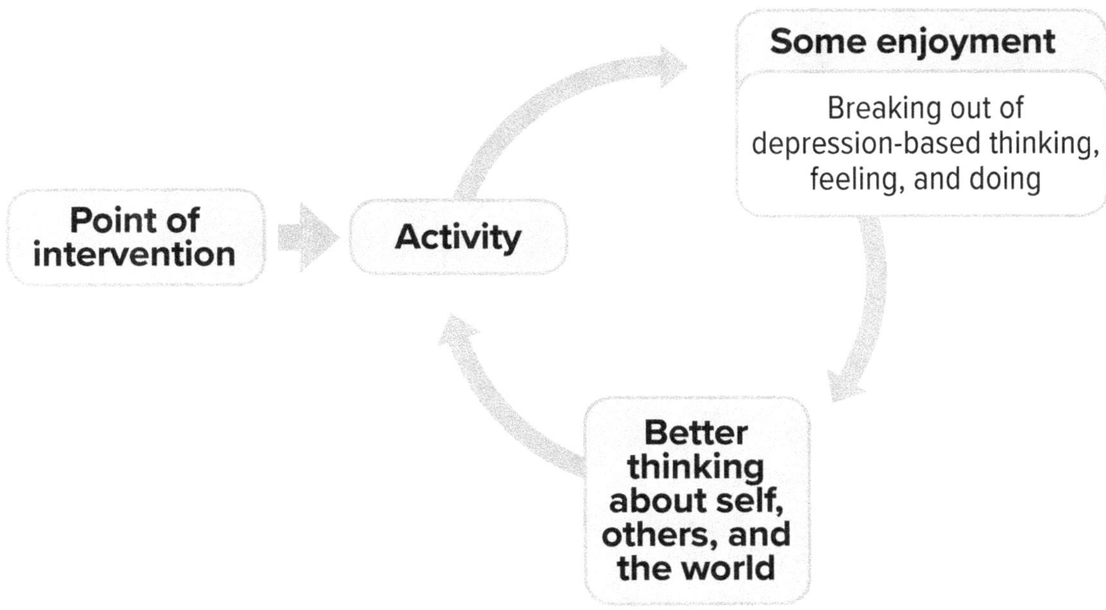

Figure 16

	Mon	Tue	Wed	Thu	Fri	Sat	Sun
Morning							
Afternoon							
Evening							

Figure 17

Automatic Thought (AT)	Evidence for AT	Evidence Against AT

Figure 20

What depression has taken away from me:	What I would like back:

Figure 22

Things I have done today:
7 AM–11 AM
11 AM–1 PM
1 PM–3 PM
3 PM–5 PM
5 PM–7 PM
7 PM–10 PM
After 10 PM

Figure 23

Most of the day I did these three things:
1
2.
3.

Figure 24

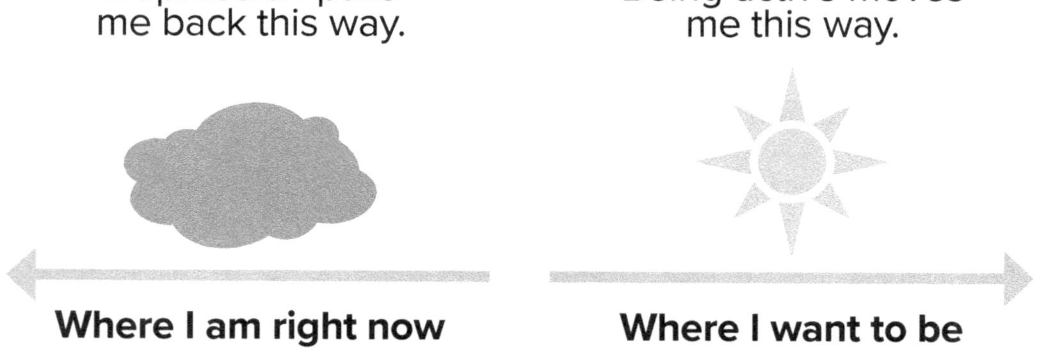

Figure 25

	Morning	Afternoon	Evening
Mon			
Tue			
Wed			
Thu			
Fri			
Sat			
Sun			

Figure 26

From *Treating Depression Using Cognitive Behavioral Therapy Skills and Interventions.* © OhioGuidestone. Owners of this book are granted permission to reproduce pages for use with their clients.

Activity Schedule for:	
Time:	

From *Treating Depression Using Cognitive Behavioral Therapy Skills and Interventions.* © OhioGuidestone. Owners of this book are granted permission to reproduce pages for use with their clients.

Figure 27

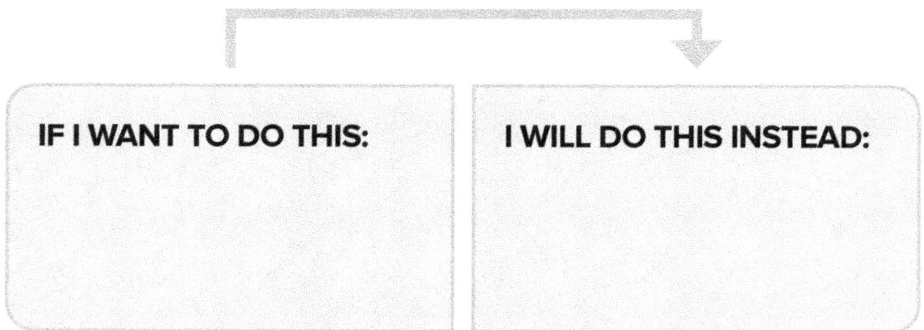

Figure 28

	Afternoon
Mon	
Tue	
Wed	
Thu	
Fri	
Sat	
Sun	

Figure 30

Today's Activities
Time:
I usually do this:
Instead I will do this:

Figure 31

Today I will move in the direction of a meaningful life.

I can do this.

One step at a time.

Today I make my life better by _________________________________

____

____

____

Figure 32

Activity	Able to Do?
Get out of chair	
Stretch while standing	
Walk around apartment/space	
Walk down flight of stairs	
Walk around the block	
Walk a mile	
. . .	

Figure 33

<table>
<tr><td colspan="8">Physical Activity "Prescription"</td></tr>
<tr><td colspan="8">Name:</td></tr>
<tr><td colspan="8">Date:</td></tr>
<tr><td colspan="8">Prescribed Activity:</td></tr>
<tr><td colspan="8">Dosage/Frequency:</td></tr>
<tr><td colspan="8">Time:</td></tr>
<tr><td>Activity Completed:</td><td></td><td></td><td></td><td></td><td></td><td></td><td></td></tr>
</table>

Figure 34

<table>
<tr><td colspan="8">Musical Activity "Prescription"</td></tr>
<tr><td colspan="8">Name:</td></tr>
<tr><td colspan="8">Date:</td></tr>
<tr><td colspan="8">Prescribed Activity:</td></tr>
<tr><td colspan="8">Dosage/Frequency:</td></tr>
<tr><td colspan="8">Time:</td></tr>
<tr><td>Activity Completed:</td><td></td><td></td><td></td><td></td><td></td><td></td><td></td></tr>
</table>

Figure 35

Art Activity "Prescription"							
Name:							
Date:							
Prescribed Activity:							
Dosage/Frequency:							
Time:							
Activity Completed:							

Figure 36

Dance Activity "Prescription"							
Name:							
Date:							
Prescribed Activity:							
Dosage/Frequency:							
Time:							
Activity Completed:							

Figure 37

Getting ready to help_____________________
Call _________
Find out what the organization needs
Determine if you are willing/able to do what is needed
Make an appointment to visit
Plan for getting there/back
Go to your first volunteer session

Figure 38

Helping Activity "Prescription"							
Name:							
Date:							
Prescribed Activity:							
Dosage/Frequency:							
Time:							
Activity Completed:							

Figure 39

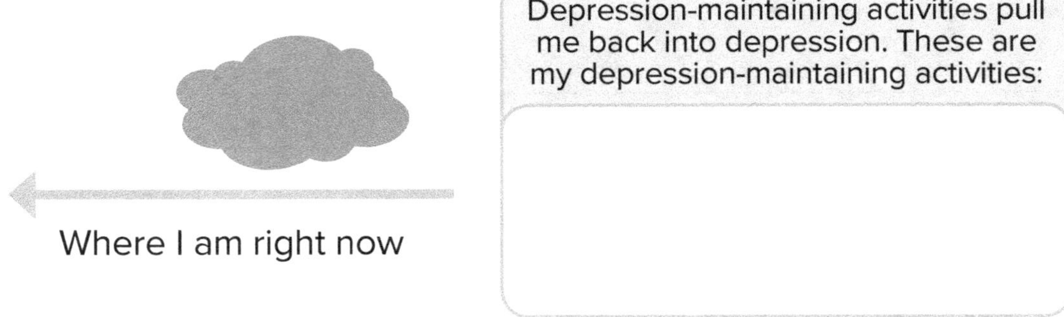

Figure 40

Meaningful Activity "Prescription"							
Name:							
Date:							
Prescribed Activity:							
Dosage/Frequency:							
Time:							
Activity Completed:							

Figure 41

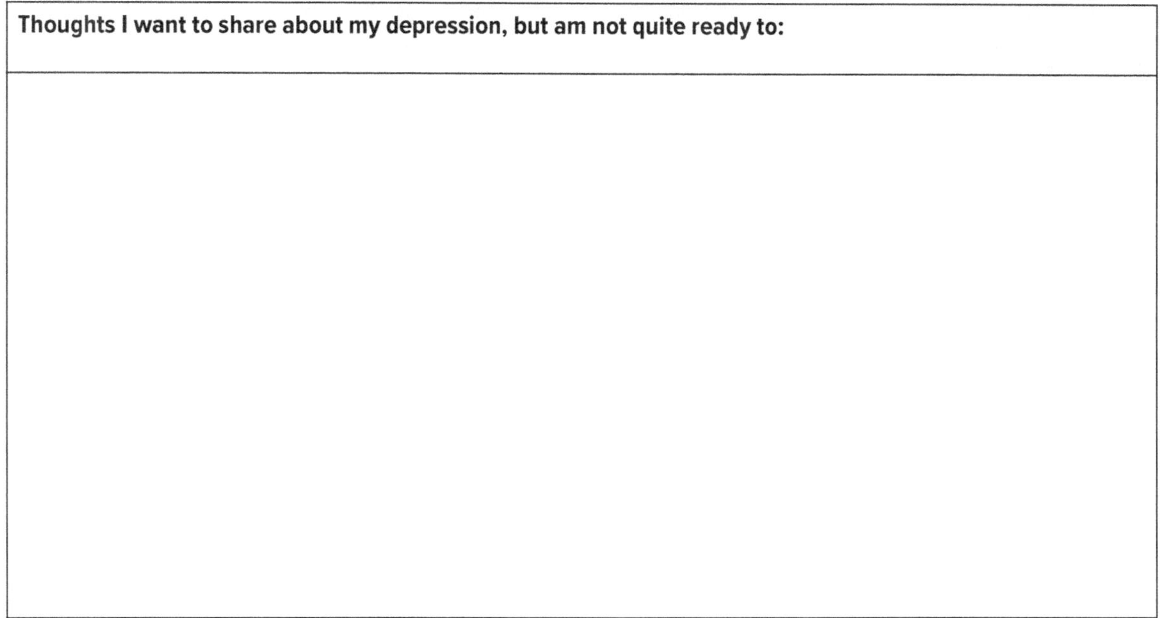

Figure 42

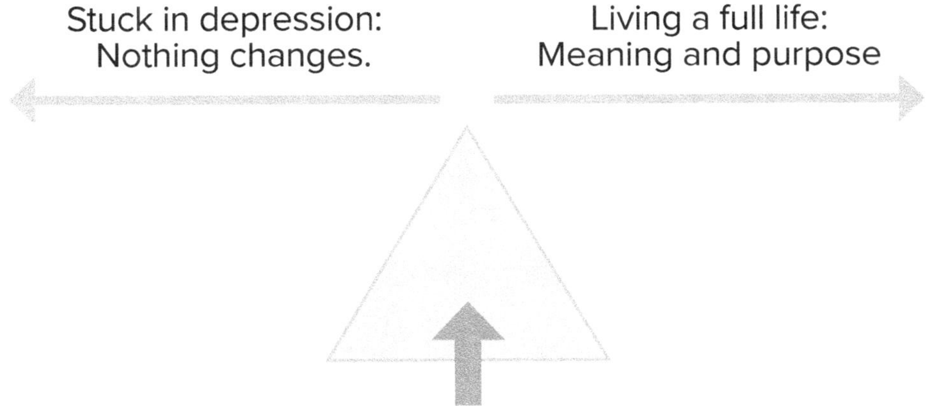

Figure 43

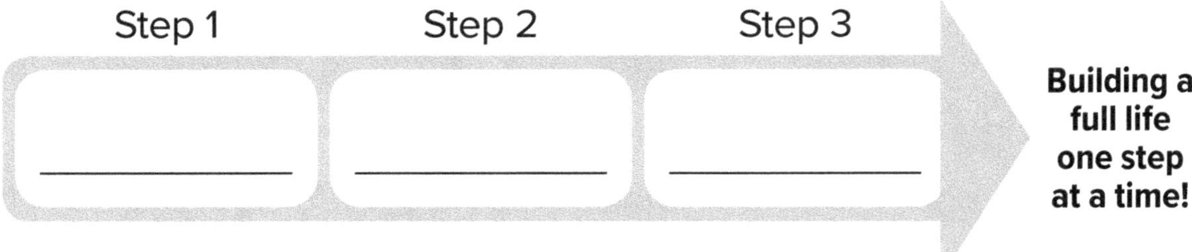

Figure 44

Mapping Out Kindness	
Completed ?	
Where?	
When?	
What will I say?	
What will I do?	

Figure 46

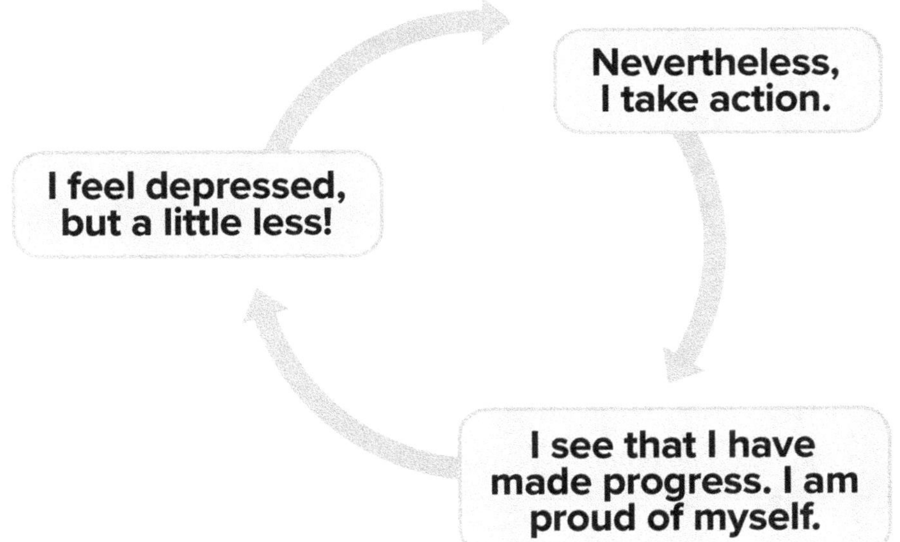

Figure 47

Figure 48

The one thing I am going to do:
Monday:
Tuesday:
Wednesday:
Thursday:
Friday:

Figure 49

From *Treating Depression Using Cognitive Behavioral Therapy Skills and Interventions*. © OhioGuidestone. Owners of this book are granted permission to reproduce pages for use with their clients.

Being kind to myself:	Done
Monday:	
Tuesday:	
Wednesday:	
Thursday:	
Friday:	

Figure 50

From *Treating Depression Using Cognitive Behavioral Therapy Skills and Interventions*. © OhioGuidestone. Owners of this book are granted permission to reproduce pages for use with their clients.

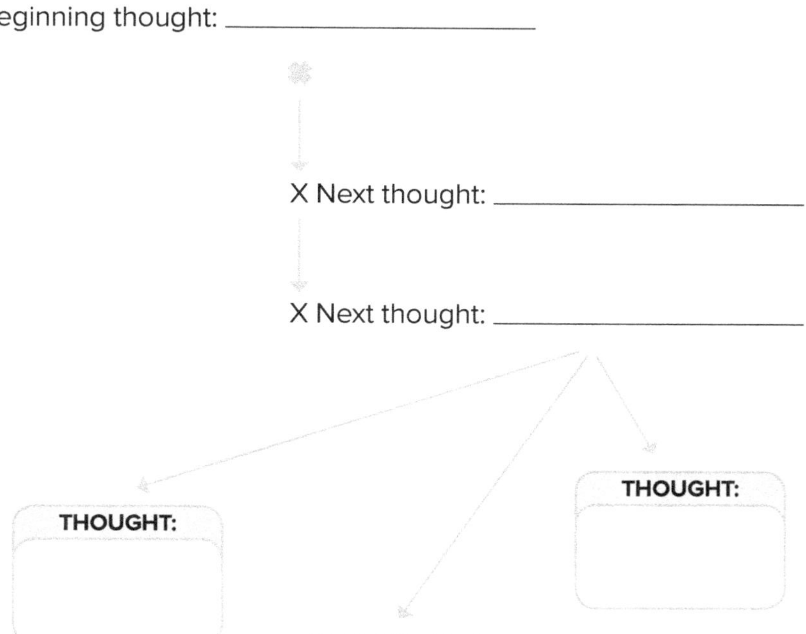

Figure 51

Figure 52

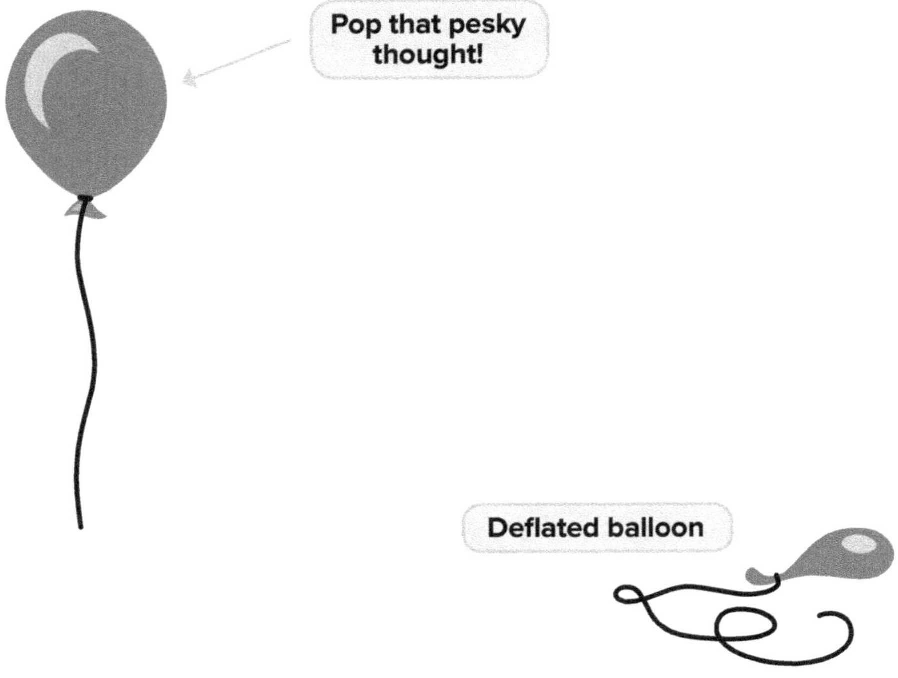

Figure 53

From *Treating Depression Using Cognitive Behavioral Therapy Skills and Interventions.* © OhioGuidestone. Owners of this book are granted permission to reproduce pages for use with their clients.

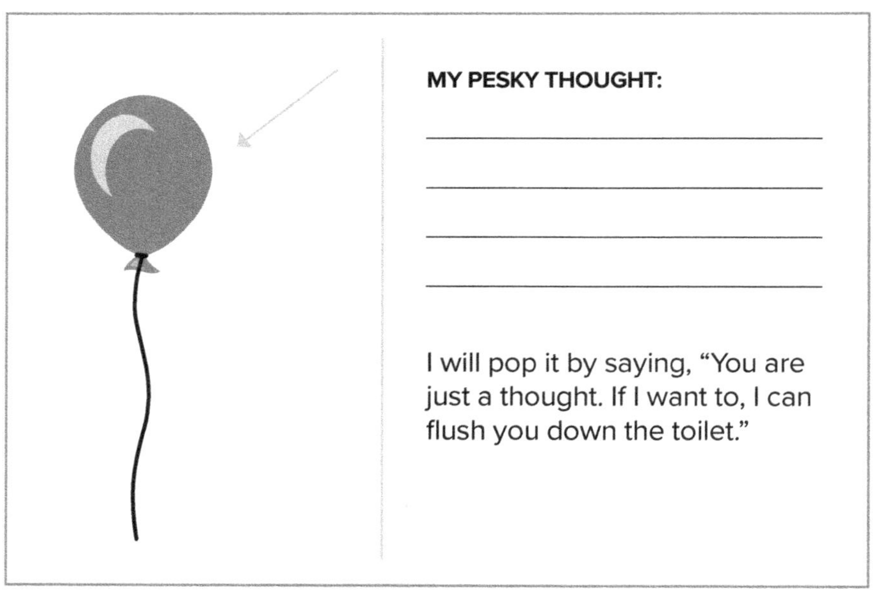

Figure 54

From *Treating Depression Using Cognitive Behavioral Therapy Skills and Interventions.* © OhioGuidestone. Owners of this book are granted permission to reproduce pages for use with their clients.

Thought:	How much is it worth?

Figure 55

	Thought:	How much is it worth?
Mon		
Tue		
Wed		
Thu		
Fri		
Sat		
Sun		

Figure 56

<table>
<tr><td>Bully Thought:</td></tr>
<tr><td>Evidence for:</td></tr>
<tr><td>

</td></tr>
<tr><td>Evidence against:</td></tr>
<tr><td>

</td></tr>
</table>

Figure 57

<table>
<tr><td>Reasons to Be:</td></tr>
<tr><td>1.</td></tr>
<tr><td>2.</td></tr>
<tr><td>3.</td></tr>
<tr><td>4.</td></tr>
<tr><td>5.</td></tr>
<tr><td>6.</td></tr>
<tr><td>7.</td></tr>
<tr><td>8.</td></tr>
<tr><td>9.</td></tr>
<tr><td>10.</td></tr>
</table>

Figure 58

I think the following things would give me joy:
I think the following things are meaningful to me:

Figure 59

Thinking Like a Wizard
If I were a wizard I would have no trouble thinking about:
If I were a wizard I would just:

Figure 60

1.What I really want:
Next steps:
2. What I also really want:
Next steps:
3. Another thing I really want:
Next steps:

Figure 61

"Going to pieces" thought:	Evidence for the thought:	Evidence against the thought:

Figure 62

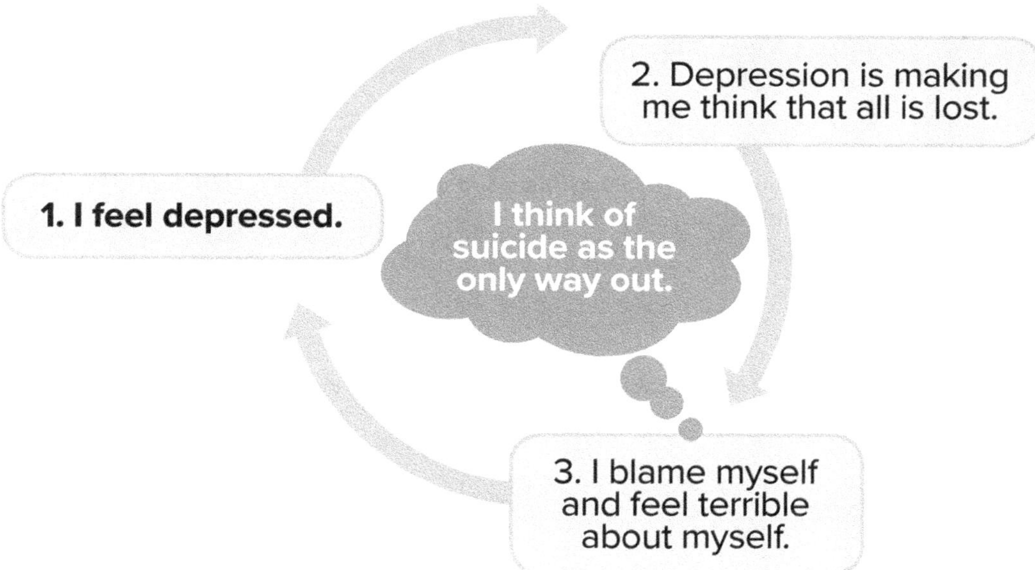

Figure 63

"Going to pieces" thought:	
Evidence for the thought:	
Evidence against the thought:	

Figure 64

My "going to pieces" thought:

____

If this thought were not true, here is what would change about how I think about myself:

If this thought were not true, here is what would change about the way I think about the world:

Figure 65

WELL DONE!
Keep up the
good work.

Figure 66

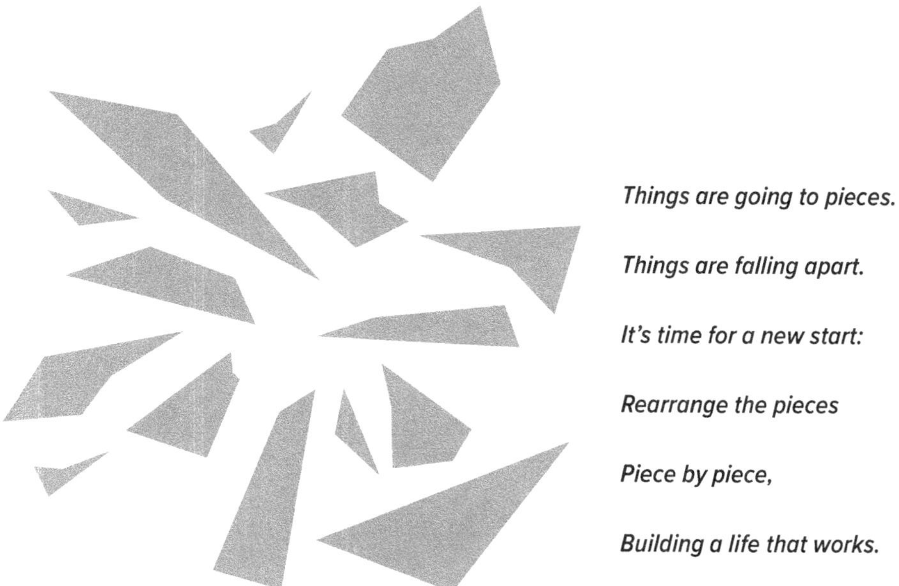

Figure 67

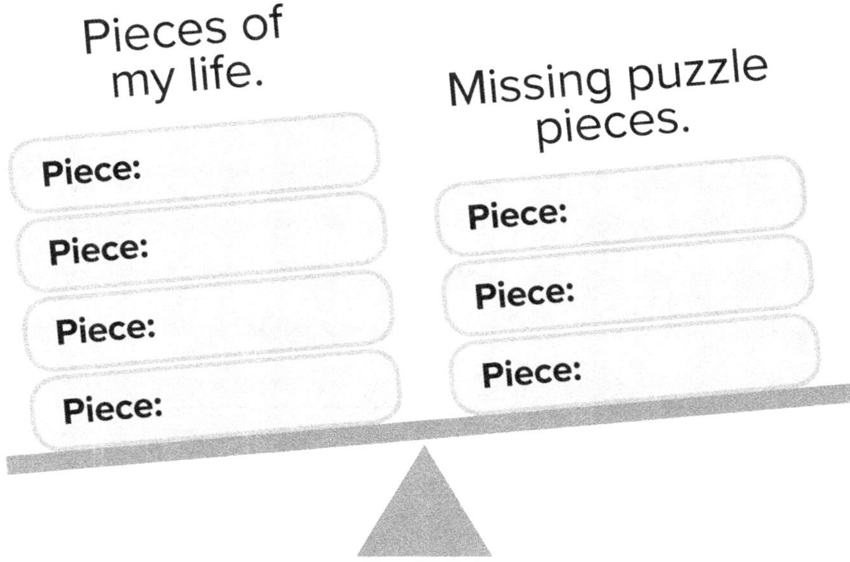

Figure 68

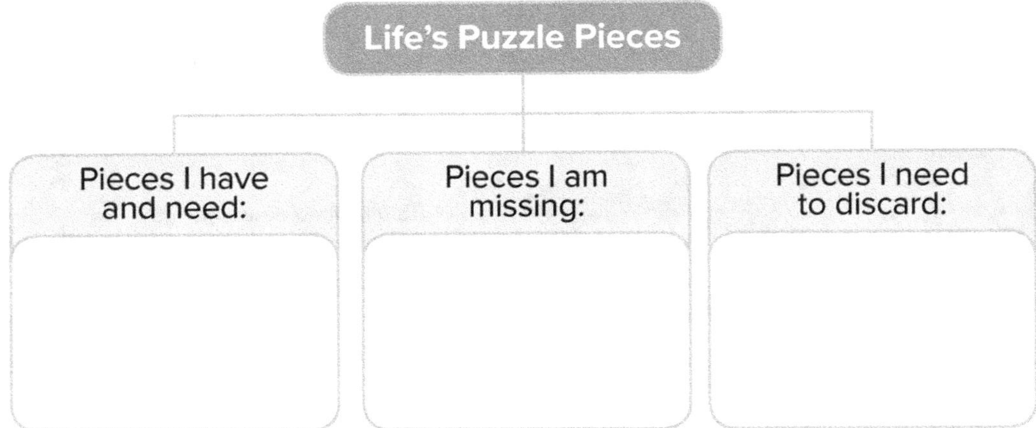

Figure 69

If life was fair I . . .
1.
2.
3.
4.
5.
6.

Figure 70

I accept that:

In spite of things being as they are, I will:

Figure 71

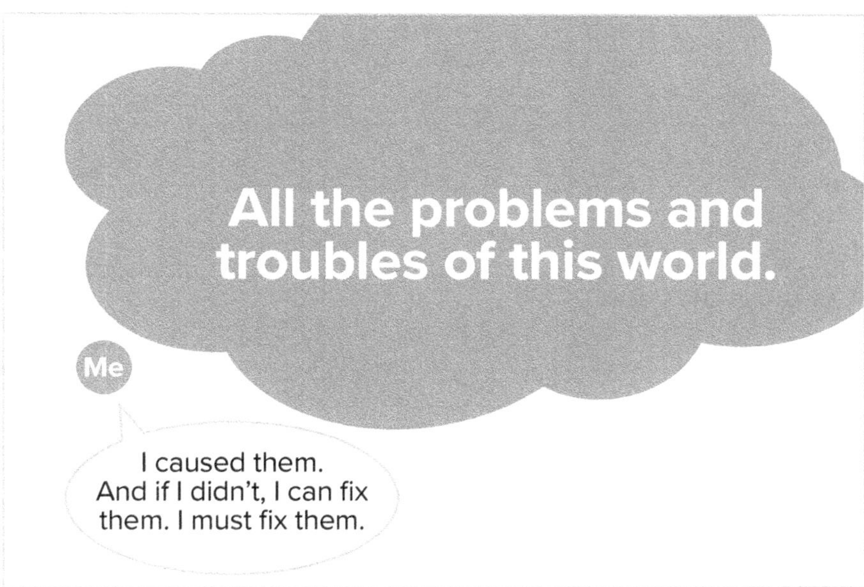

Figure 72

Figure 73

Is this about me?
Did I cause the situation?
Is it for me to try to resolve the situation?
If I did not cause the situation and it is not for me to resolve it: I stay away from it. I move on.

Figure 74

<table>
<tr><td>I should:</td></tr>
<tr><td></td></tr>
<tr><td></td></tr>
<tr><td></td></tr>
<tr><td></td></tr>
<tr><td></td></tr>
</table>

Figure 75

I should...

I really want to...

Figure 76

ASSUMPTION:

Jack wants me to do the laundry
because I see it piled in front of the washer.

ACTION:

I do the laundry.

PROBLEM:

Jack wanted to sort the laundry when he got home.
Colors are all mixed. Jack is upset with me.

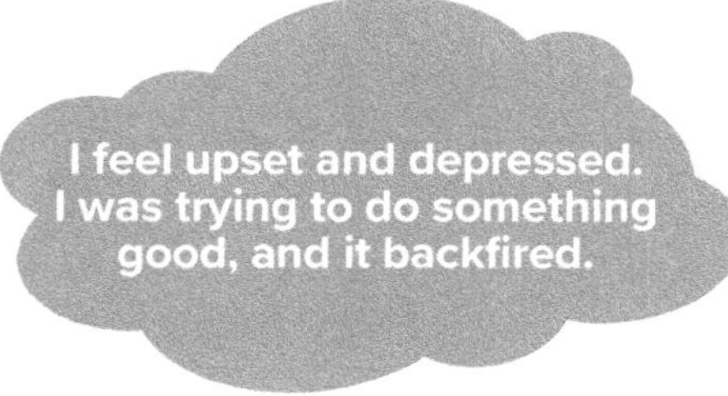

Figure 77

When in doubt:

Simply ask!

What are you thinking?

What do you need/want?

Figure 78

My Thought Support Team

1.

4.

____________'s Team

2.

3.

Figure 79

PESKY AUTOMATIC THOUGHT:

What _____________ would say about this:

How I would feel if I believed this:

What _____________ would say about this:

How I would feel if I believed this:

What _____________ would say about this:

How I would feel if I believed this:

Figure 80

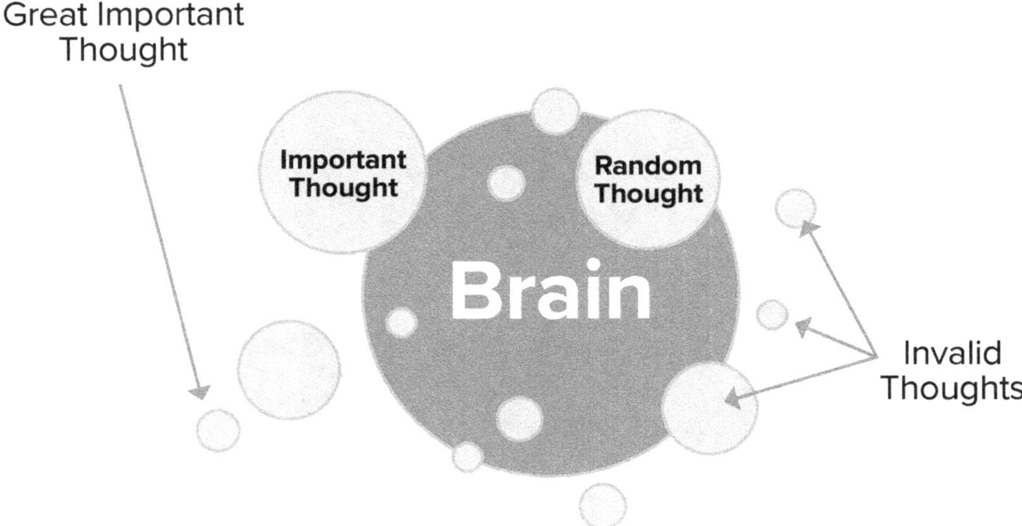

Figure 81

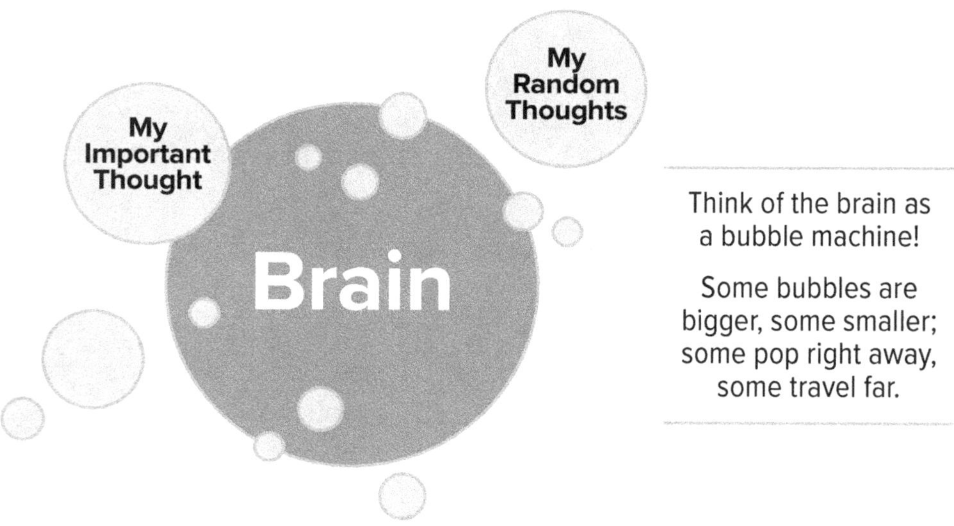

Figure 82

Thought about Treatment?	What Kind of Thought?

Figure 83

Beginning:	Now:

Figure 84

I know I think better because:	I know I feel better because:	I know I do better because:

Figure 85

I am done with treatment if/when . . .	What kind of a thought is this?

Figure 86

Figure 87

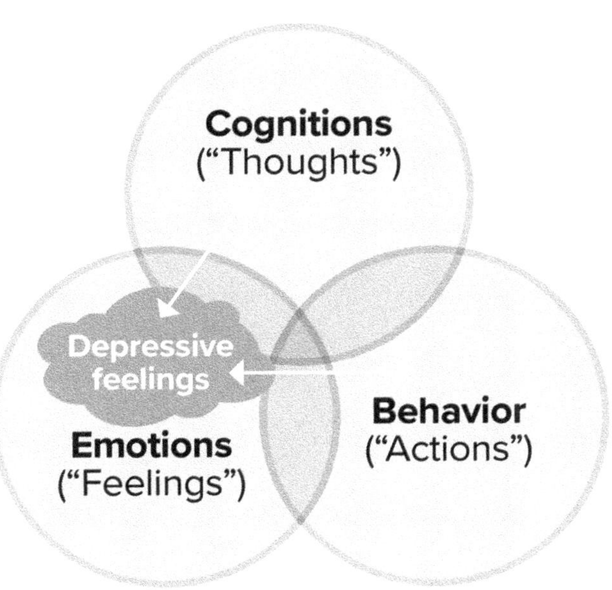

Figure 88

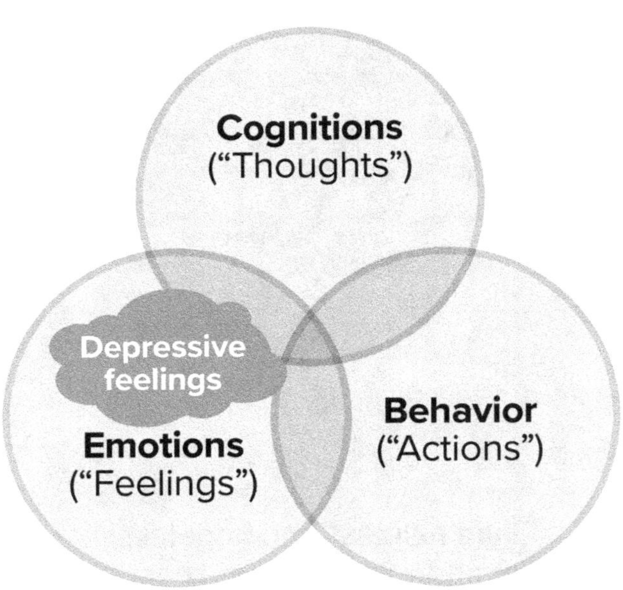

Figure 89

Figure 90

Figure 91

Depressive feeling:	What is this feeling telling me?	Is what the feeling is telling me actually true?

Figure 92

From *Treating Depression Using Cognitive Behavioral Therapy Skills and Interventions.* © OhioGuidestone. Owners of this book are granted permission to reproduce pages for use with their clients.

Depressive feeling:	What is this feeling telling me?	Evidence against the message the feeling is giving me:	Is what the feeling is telling me actually true?

Figure 93

From *Treating Depression Using Cognitive Behavioral Therapy Skills and Interventions.* © OhioGuidestone. Owners of this book are granted permission to reproduce pages for use with their clients.

Name:

Difficult Feeling:

How _________________ interacts with the message
the difficult feeling sends:

Figure 94

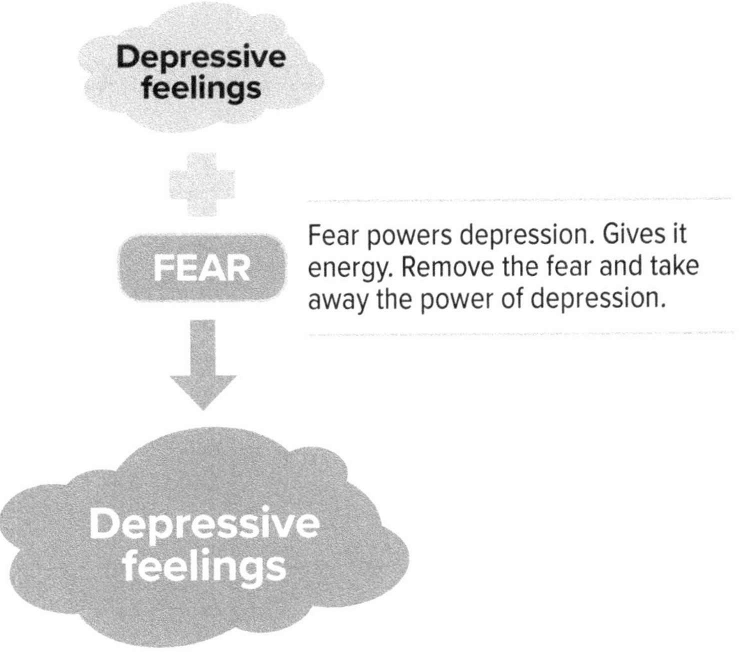

Figure 95

Figure 96

Ways in which my depressive feelings are protective:	Ways in which they keep me from fully participating in life:

Figure 97

The thing/person I feel curious about:	Ways in which I can follow the feeling of curiosity and experience the thing I am curious about:

Figure 98

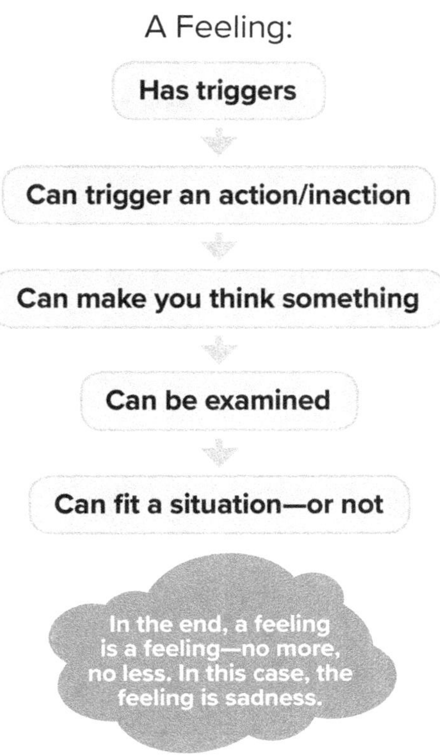

Figure 99

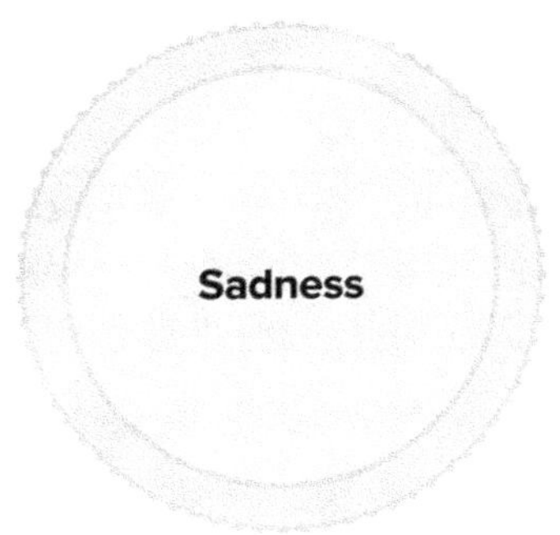

Cut out the coin shapes and glue
them together, letters facing outward.

Figure 100

Parts of my meaningful and connected life:	Everyday steps I can take to get there:

Figure 101

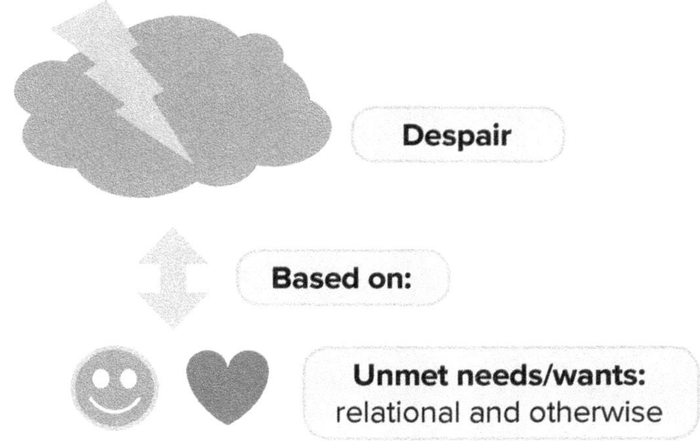

THE BOTTOM LINE:
Move toward meeting needs
and wants in order to move away
from feelings of despair.

Figure 102

Complete despair   **Very meaningful life**

Small steps—creating meaning and connection.

Figure 103

Figure 104

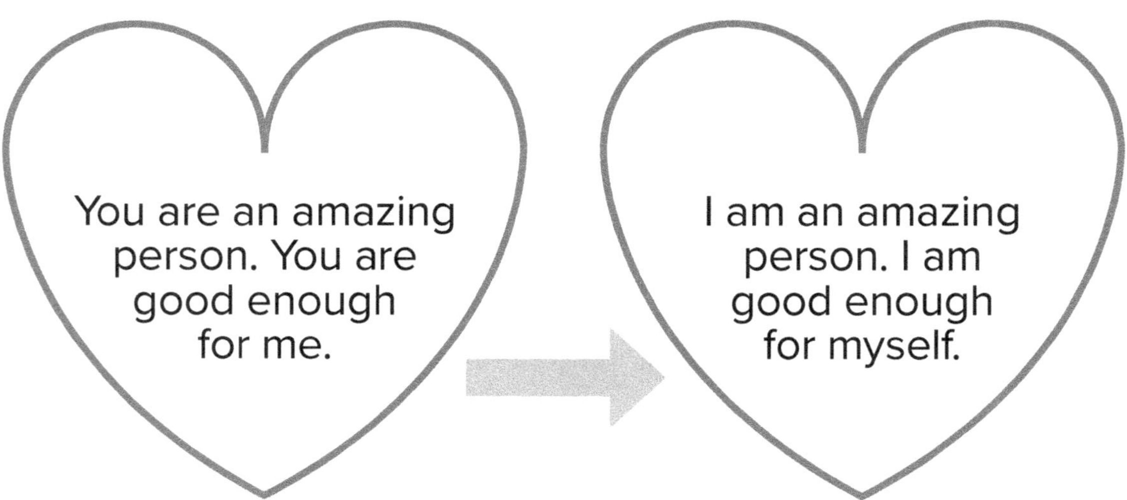

Figure 105

Figure 106

References

ACES too high (2017). ACES too high website. Retrieved from https://acestoohigh.com/aces-101/.

American Psychiatric Association. (2013). *Diagnostic and statistical manual of mental disorders* (5th ed.). Arlington, VA: Author.

Beck, A.T., Rush, A. J., Shaw, B. F., & Emery, G. (1979). *Cognitive therapy of depression.* New York: Guilford Press.

Davis, K. L., Panksepp, J., & Solms, M. (2018). *The emotional foundations of personality: A neurobiological and evolutionary approach.* New York: Norton.

Dobson, D., & Dobson, K. (2017). *Evidence-based practice of cognitive behavioral therapy* (2nd ed.). New York: Guilford Press.

Fefergrad, M., & Zaretsky, A. (2013). *Cognitive behavioral therapy for depression.* New York: Norton.

Fisher, J. E. , & O'Donohue, W. (2006). *The practitioner's guide to evidence-based psychotherapy.* New York: Springer.

Jong, P. D., & Berg, I. K. (2013). *Interviewing for solutions.* South Melbourne, Australia: Brooks/Cole, Cengage Learning.

Narvaez, D. (2014). *Neurobiology and the development of human morality: Evolution, culture, and wisdom.* New York: Norton.

Persons, J. B., Davidson, J., & Tompkins, M. A. (2001). *Essential components of cognitive-behavior therapy for depression.* Washington, DC: American Psychological Association.

Schore, A. N. (2016). *Affect regulation and the origin of the self: The neurobiology of emotional development.* New York: Psychology Press.

Schore, J. R., & Schore, A. N. (2008). Modern attachment theory: The central role of affect regulation in development and treatment. *Clinical Social Work Journal , 36,* 9–20. DOI: 10.1007/s10615-007-0111-7

Tolin, D. F. (2016). *Doing CBT: A comprehensive guide to working with behaviors, thoughts, and emotions.* New York: Guilford Press.